BRINGING THE MONTESSORI APPROACH TO YOUR EARLY YEARS PRACTICE

Also available:

Bringing the High/Scope Approach to your Early Years Practice
Nicky Holt
978-1-84312-431-3
1-84312-431-9

Bringing the Reggio Approach to your Early Years Practice
Pat Brunton and Linda Thornton
978-1-84312-430-6
1-84312-430-0

Bringing the Steiner Waldorf Approach to your Early Years Practice
Janni Nicol
978-1-84312-433-7
1-84312-433-5

BRINGING THE MONTESSORI APPROACH TO YOUR EARLY YEARS PRACTICE

Barbara Isaacs

Routledge
Taylor & Francis Group

LONDON AND NEW YORK

First published 2007
by Routledge
2 Park Square, Milton Park, Abingdon, Oxon OX14 4RN

Simultaneously published in the USA and Canada
by Routledge
270 Madison Ave, New York, NY 10016

Routledge is an imprint of the Taylor & Francis Group, an informa business

© 2007 Barbara Isaacs

British Library Cataloguing in Publication Data
A catalogue record for this book is available from the British Library

Library of Congress Cataloging in Publication Data
A catalog record for this book has been requested

ISBN10: 1–84312–432–7
ISBN13: 978–1–84312–432–0

Designed and typeset in Helvetica by FiSH Books, Enfield, Middx
Printed and bound in Great Britain by TJ International Ltd, Padstow, Cornwall

Contents

Acknowledgements

Barbara Isaacs would like to thank the children and staff at Seedlings Montessori Nursery, Wantage and her friends and colleagues at Montessori Centre International for giving her the opportunity to continue learning from them. Special thanks go also to her husband and children for their continued support and encouragement.

Introduction

In January 2007 we will celebrate the centenary of the opening of the first Montessori nursery in Rome. I hope this book will extend awareness of the unique nature of this event and will help to explain the reasons why it remains so relevant to the lives of today's children, their parents and carers, and also the communities in which they live.

There is no doubt that Maria Montessori's pedagogy has made an impact on today's understanding of early years education and has influenced present-day good practice. That this contribution is not always recognised or attributed to Montessori may lie in the fact that, over the years and through the rapid expansion of early years services, we have often forgotten to reflect on and appreciate the roots from which the early years community has grown. The work of Friedrich Wilhelm Froebel, Rudolf Steiner, the Macmillan sisters and Susan Isaacs forms the foundation of our understanding of nursery education in today's Britain and highlights the need for an informed pedagogy that continues to evolve. Montessori herself refers in her writing to the work of Jean-Jacques Rousseau and Friedrich Wilhelm Froebel, as well as to two French educationalists, Edouard Seguin and Jean-Marc-Gaspard Itard. From her earliest writing Montessori also makes links with developmental theorists of the day, such as Sigmund Freud and Jean Piaget. Tina Bruce makes a clear case for this considered approach:

> Until we are clear about the lenses through which we view children, we cannot begin to work effectively with them, nor is it easy to work in partnership with other practitioners or multi-agency colleagues, parents or carers, because our assumptions about the child are crucial in influencing our practice.

(Bruce, 2005:2)

The Montessori approach is possibly best known today for the contribution it makes to our understanding of the importance of learning through the senses and the development of learning materials that are today referred to as 'educational toys', a new concept in Montessori's time. However, we need to understand that the materials, or apparatus as they were called by Montessori, are tools for children to reveal their 'true nature'. I believe that the key to the continued success of the Montessori approach lies in the unique relationship between the respect and trust in the child's ability to construct themself within a 'favourable environment'. According to Montessori, this favourable environment offers children the opportunity to learn by following the unique rhythm of each child and being supported by sensitive, well-prepared adults who respect the child's individuality. However, Montessori also highlights the important contribution all children make to our future and sees children as agents for potential social change through her vision of 'Education for Peace'. This vision is an essential part of her evolutionary approach to the education of children, which she called 'Cosmic Education'.

I hope this book will help to unravel some of the complex terminology Montessori uses and will make her writing more accessible to today's readers. It is important to see Montessori's writing from a historical perspective: most of her books consist of a series of lectures, speeches and presentations that were edited into books more than fifty years ago, and were translated from Italian. Her use of language seems somewhat archaic now and changes in our understanding and use of certain terms has contributed to uncertainty and controversy over her exact meaning, as for example when she refers to deviations or the normalisation of the child. In addition, some of the terminology used in the last century is provocative to the readers of today, such as Montessori's reference (1964 [1912]) to 'working with idiot children'. Nonetheless, the spirit of the child and her commitment to following the child remain constant throughout Montessori's writing, as does her reverence for children and her understanding that children hold our future in their hands.

Chapter 1
Background

Maria Montessori's early life and study

Maria Montessori's own life is closely linked with the political, social and economic changes that resulted from the unification of Italy in the year Montessori was born, 1870. The political change also heralded social and economic change but the process was slow as was inevitable in a country with a male-dominated electoral minority, large levels of illiteracy, and driven by the Catholic church. The economic and social status of the population contributed to the continued struggle within Italian society. The division between the small group of wealthy and educated people and the large peasant population continued to undermine the political movement and ultimately led to the emergence of the fascist state led by Benito Mussolini. So this was the Italy into which Maria Montessori was born in Chiaravalle in the province of Ancona on 31 August 1870.

Maria was the only daughter of Alessandro Montessori and Renilde Stoppani. Alessandro's nationalistic and somewhat conservative outlook on life contrasted with the progressive and liberal Renilde, who was unusually well educated for a girl born within the region. As a civil servant Alessandro and his family were expected to move home many times. They finally settled in Rome in 1875, when Maria was five years old. This gave the family the opportunity to join the city's growing middle classes where they had access to the culture and intellectual energy of this growing capital.

Maria joined the public school in Via de San Nicola da Tolentino at the age of six, in 1876, the year before primary education had become compulsory in Italy. Anecdotes from devoted friends paint a picture of a determined and diligent young girl, untypical of her social class. Montessori preferred to follow the technical, rather than the classical stream of education, reflected in her interest and love of mathematics and the opportunity taken to follow the 'modern curriculum' (Kramer, 1976:32).

By the time Montessori graduated at the age of twenty she was interested in biological sciences and was determined to study medicine, a path not followed by a woman in Italy before. Having achieved the Diploma de License in the spring of 1892 with the high grade of 8 out of 10, Montessori was eligible to study medicine at the University of Rome. In her day it was unthinkable for a woman to join the medical faculty, where all the facilities were designed for men. It is not clear what intervention Montessori used to achieve her goal, but the fact is that in 1892 she did join the University as a medical student.

Montessori's years of study were challenging in every aspect: her father disapproved, she was ridiculed by her fellow students and she also hated dissection, which she had to perform in the evenings. In 1894 she won the Roti prize and the scholarship that accompanied it. By 1896 she started working both with children and women as well as attending the Regia psychiatric clinic. In the last year of her studies, like the rest of her fellow students, she gave a lecture to the class. She expected to be ridiculed, instead her talk was well attended and received and there was an extra bonus, it was attended by her father. Montessori's success had ended six years of rejection and criticism. She was much admired and celebrated. Montessori herself wrote to a friend in 1896: 'So here I am: famous!... I am not famous because of my skill or intelligence, but for my courage and indifference.... This is something which, if one wishes, one can always achieve, but it takes tremendous effort.'

In the same year Montessori started her first appointment as the surgical assistant at San Spirito's hospital. She also helped in children's and women's hospitals and established her own private practice. Like many nineteenth-century women of her class, she felt social responsibility for the poor and supported them far beyond the duty expected from a physician. In 1897 she was asked to visit Rome's asylums, and this led to meeting the 'idiot children' who were to change her life. Montessori's experience of these children collecting crumbs from the floor once they had eaten had led her to consider the fact that perhaps they behaved in this way because they were bored. They had nothing to play with!

Montessori continued to be preoccupied with the fate of these children in the asylum and her encounter with the work of Jean-Marc-Gaspard Itard (born 1775) and his pupil Edouard Seguin (born 1812) gave some answers. Itard was and is best known for his study of the Wild Boy of Aveyron, a feral child, who was discovered running wild in the Aveyron wood. He decided to 'civilise the young man', to develop his senses and to gradually teach him to speak. Itard developed his own method for promoting the boy's language skills based on sensorial experiences and matching, pairing and sorting activities. Many of these teaching tools were to be used and developed by Montessori a hundred years later when she came to work with children in the first Casa dei Bambini, in the San Lorenzo district of Rome.

Montessori also found inspiration in Edouard Seguin's work, which led her to believe 'that mental deficiency presented chiefly a pedagogical rather than medical problem' (Kramer, 1976:96). In the spring of 1900 The National League for Retarded Children opened the medical-pedagogical institute, a school for what we call today children with special needs. Montessori became the director with twenty-two children attending.

One of Montessori's co-directors of the institute, Dr Montessano, gradually became a close friend and lover. The result of this union was a son, Mario. Kramer (1976:92) says: 'Everything we know about her makes it unbelievable that it could have been a casual liaison.' Mario was given his mother's name and went to a wet nurse after birth. It is hard to imagine the psychological impact this event had on Dr Montessori. At the beginning of the twentieth century having a child out of wedlock would have been professional as well as social suicide. 'Deprived of the experience of caring for her own child, she was to turn her attention increasingly to meeting the needs of other children' (Kramer, 1976:93).

In 1900, Montessori again enrolled to study at the University of Rome. She continued her interest in psychology and pursued Seguin's theory of educating the senses through concrete experiences. In Naples in 1902 she presented her own ideas about the possibility of the education of 'unteachable children'. She made links between the two theories exploring the notion of training of the senses and the importance of approaching abstraction through concrete forms a child could see and touch (Kramer, 1976). This was the basis for later development of the Montessori apparatus and sensorial materials that she called 'materialised abstractions'.

One of her students of the time and a later friend and collaborator was Anna Maccheroni, who recalled (in Kramer, 1976:97–98) Montessori's lectures: 'She was a most attractive lecturer; her language was so simple, so clear, her delivery so animated, that even the poorer students could understand her. All that she said had the warmth of life.'

The first Montessori nursery

In 1906 Montessori was asked to look after children of migrant workers who lived in the tenements of the San Lorenzo district of Rome. The rationale for the project was simple: while the parents worked and older children attended school, the three to six year olds roamed the streets and got up to mischief. The developers who owned the tenements decided to contain these children in a room and invited Dr Montessori to take charge of them. As the funding for this project was non-existent, Montessori furnished the room with small tables and chairs rather than desks, a selection of modified materials originally used with her 'idiot children', and she employed the porter's daughter to look after these fifty or so street urchins. Two of the revolutionary classrooms were set up and Montessori herself was actively involved for two years. Her work with those children laid a foundation for what we know today as the Montessori approach to education.

The first Casa dei Bambini opened in 58 Via dei Marsai, San Lorenzo, Rome on 6 January 1907. From the beginning Montessori observed the children's reactions to their new environment without any pre-conceived ideas of what would happen. These observations provided opportunities to understand better the children and the materials themselves – this was, what we call today, action research. She modified the materials in relation to the children's use, adapting them further for the use of children without learning difficulties. Montessori's observations gave her a further insight into the nature of children and formed the basis of the discoveries explained in her first book *The Montessori Method*, which was published in Rome in 1912. In this book Montessori described children as:

- being capable of extended periods of concentration;

- enjoying repetition and order;

- revelling in the freedom of movement and choice;

- enjoying purposeful activities (preferred work to play);

- self-motivated, displaying behaviours that did not require either punishments or rewards;

- taking delight in silence and harmony of the environment;

- possessing personal dignity and spontaneous self-discipline;

- being capable of learning to read and write.

It was these discoveries that made Montessori believe that these characteristics represented the potential of humanity. She advocated that all children should be given the opportunity to 'reveal themselves' in a developmentally appropriate environment that would facilitate their natural growth and development.

Both E.M. Standing (1984) and Rita Kramer (1976) document the history of the rise of the Montessori approach in great detail in their books. Both authors give a unique insight into this social and pedagogical experiment that Montessori herself described as follows on the occasion of the opening of the second Children's House:

> This is not simply a place where the children are kept, ... but a true school for their education. ... We have put the school within the home ... We have placed it within the home as the property of the community ... The idea of the community ownership of the school is new and very beautiful and profoundly educational. The parents know that the Casa dei Bambini is their property and is maintained by a portion of the rent they pay. Mothers can go at any hour of the day to watch ...

> (Montessori in Kramer, 1976:123)

For Montessori the Casa dei Bambini was a tool for social change for both children and their mothers and in this inaugural speech she also related to maternal functions and the need and opportunities for women to work and have their children in care of 'the directress [Montessori's name for the teacher] and the house physician' (Kramer, 1976:124). Here Kramer expresses her view that Montessori may possibly reflect on her own 'inability to mother her child' and her concern for the quality of care to be given to children of absent mothers. This dilemma continues to haunt today's working mothers.

There is no doubt that the children thrived and parents appreciated their children's growing awareness of hygiene, good manners, as well as independence and opportunities to learn. The reputation of this pedagogical experiment spread rapidly thanks to growing affordability of newsprint. Within the next two years the Children's Houses had many Italian and foreign visitors with dignitaries and teachers coming from all over the world.

International Montessori Movement

Montessori decided in 1913 to give up both her lectureship at the University and in the medical profession, from then on she would devote her energies to the training of Montessori teachers, to the development of

Montessori learning materials and to the establishment of the Montessori network worldwide. Between 1907 and 1914, when World War 1 broke out, interest in Montessori education flourished and many opportunities were opened to Montessori to promote her unique view of children and their learning. By 1914 there were hundreds of Montessori schools established in Europe, North and South America as well as India, Sri Lanka and Pakistan.

For the next forty years Montessori continued to travel, lecture and promote Montessori education. She visited all the continents and left us a legacy from which thousands and thousands of children around the globe benefited. She died in the Netherlands at the end of the summer of 1952 wanting to be known as a citizen of the world.

Chapter 2

The Montessori approach

The Montessori Method of Education has three key components:

- the child;
- the favourable environment;
- the teacher.

The relationship between the child, teacher and environment continues to evolve and develop because it is based on observation of children. The dynamic links between all three components and their interaction represent what we know today as the Montessori approach.

The child

Montessori recognises and celebrates the unique individuality of each child and the potential that they hold within themselves. She urges adults to demonstrate trust in the child's ability to learn and absorb the culture in which they grow up and so become an adult. She saw the child as the possible agent in affecting social change on this planet.

Montessori believed that children developed in stages or planes and that each stage had its own unique qualities and characteristics. They had to be reflected in the environment and in the strategies employed by the adults when facilitating the children's learning.

Each stage is heralded by physical changes in the body, particularly of the teeth: loss of milk teeth around six, loss of molars at around twelve and emergence of wisdom teeth around the age of eighteen, when adulthood begins. The three stages are:

- the absorbent mind – conception to six (birth to three: unconscious absorbent mind; three to six: conscious absorbent mind);

- childhood – six to twelve (considered to be calm and conducive to learning);

- adolescence – twelve to eighteen (twelve to fifteen is as unpredictable as the first stage).

The age bands are approximate and provide very flexible developmental guidelines while recognising the uniqueness of each child.

The absorbent mind

The absorbent mind is a time of enormous potential in the development of the individual. Human beings need stimulation and opportunity to develop the brain through active learning and exploration, and refinement through our senses. The fundamental principle of this stage is recognition of the child as a spontaneous learner, driven by an inner drive/energy that Montessori termed 'horme'. The Greek word refers to the child's drive from within to learn from the environment – what Bruce (2005) refers to as self-motivation.

Characteristic of the absorbent mind are three embryonic stages, or as Montessori (1988a) puts it, 'periods of rebirth':

- physical embryo – when the child's physical body is formed in the womb, the pre-natal stage of life;

- spiritual embryo – the period after birth, when the unique nature of the human being, individual to each child, emerges. Montessori often talks of the child's personality in relation to this embryonic stage;

- social embryo – when the child is ready to embrace the social aspects of their life, gradually becoming aware of the social conventions of their culture and of the needs and feelings of others.

During the first stage of life we see children are predisposed to acquire certain skills and abilities during 'sensitive periods'. There are six key sensitive periods for:

- movement;

- language;

- order;

- small detail;

- refinement of the senses;

■ the social aspects of everyday life.

It is the manifestations of the sensitive periods for which the prime carer or teacher should look as they observe, so that they can provide appropriate learning opportunities for the child. Montessori believed that if this support from the adult is not available opportunities will be lost or the child will miss out on developing to their full potential. Sensitive periods are universal, evident in all children around the world. They are also present within the child at birth and can be concurrent and 'run parallel to each other'. Every sensitive period reaches its peak at a different time during the first six years of life. For example the sensitive period for language starts in the womb, when the baby recognises their mother's voice. Babies are 'pre-wired' to respond to human language. They listen attentively before their first word is uttered. Then between eighteen and thirty-six months the child's language unfolds and explodes, from passive to active vocabulary, ability to use grammar and syntax, using language appropriately within the social context.

The sensitive period for order is evident from birth and reflects the baby's need for routines that provide predictability and security for the infant. As the child grows, they will be able to orientate themselves within the home through the familiar arrangements and the child will adapt to them. For example when going for a walk we may be surprised by the toddler's ability to 'find the way' to the public library. It is their sensitive period for order that helps them to absorb the route we have taken on many previous occasions when visiting the library. By the time they are two/two and half they will be able to find toys in their room and be also able to replace them where found. The external order will be supporting their initiative, as well as organisational skills and problem solving. These are just two of the above-mentioned sensitive periods.

Montessori also describes the absorbent mind as operating at

■ the 'unconscious level' in the first three years of life, when the children are absorbing indiscriminately from the environment that surrounds them; and

■ the 'conscious level' reflecting the child's growing ability to organise and classify information, experiences and concepts. This stage of the absorbent mind is closely linked with the child's sensitive period for refinement of the senses and social aspects of life. It is supported by the sensitive periods for order and small details.

Childhood

This is the second stage of the child's development, which Montessori defined as the calm stage when the child is very keen to learn and eager to belong to a group. The characteristic sensitive periods exhibited during this plane relate to the child's moral development and acquisition of culture. (Note that from Montessori's point of view culture includes all natural sciences as well as history and geography).

Adolescence

This third plane of development is seen by Montessori as comparable with the first stage of life, with its turbulence and unpredictability and volatility. It is further subdivided into puberty (twelve to fifteen years of age), when Montessori acknowledges the big physical changes that take place within the child's body and likens it to the time of the spiritual embryo when adults need to exercise a great deal of patience and understanding in support of children of this age. The second sub-stage of this period is termed adolescence (from fifteen to eighteen); here Montessori highlights the young person's need to find a group of friends to identify with. Her revolutionary views for the education of this age group can be found in a chapter entitled 'Erdkinder', in her book *From Childhood to Adolescence.* Montessori teachers in the United States and Sweden have developed her ideas further and David Khan has written extensively on this topic for the North American Montessori Association.

Montessori also refers to a fourth stage of development that relates to the early stages of adulthood (eighteen to twenty-four years of age); however, she does not discuss any new or significant insights into the lives of young adults. In this book I will focus on children between birth and the age of six in the absorbent mind plane of development, with particular emphasis on the second stage of this plane, the three to six year olds.

The favourable environment

Rationale for the favourable environment

Montessori, just like Piaget (1962), saw the environment as a key factor in children's spontaneous learning. She believed it should be favourable to the development of the whole child, and should offer opportunities for the development of the potential of each individual.

When Montessori described the favourable environment she saw the child as an active agent of this environment and the teacher as the facilitator of the child's development. It is the role of the teacher to ensure that the environment provides for the developmental needs of each individual child; observation serves as the key tool for establishing these developmental needs.

As the child responds to the stimuli within a given environment, be it home, school or nursery, the adults present should observe and interpret behaviour according to the developmental stage of the child. With this in mind, they should ensure that the activities, materials, objects and occupations in the environment are brought to the attention of the child to facilitate, scaffold and extend developmental opportunities for the child. Adults, as well as the child's peers, act to some extent as a catalyst in the maturation process while the materials, objects and occupations within the environment scaffold the child's learning (see the work of Bruner (1960) and Vygotsky (1978) for more detail about scaffolding).

Qualities of the favourable environment

Now that we have looked at Montessori's view of the characteristics of children in different age groups, we can examine the Montessori favourable environment. This environment must be above all safe for the child. Here the nursery will follow given government guidelines, and in the British context, Ofsted's (2005) National Standards will have to be followed by every nursery.

The favourable environment is characterised by:

- accessibility and availability;
- freedom of movement and choice;
- personal responsibility;
- reality and nature;
- beauty and harmony.

Accessibility and availability

The first Children's House was designed as the house of children. Therefore everything in the rooms is prepared with children in mind. Some aspects of the environment such as the lack of desks and a teacher's table, and the child-friendly size of the furniture, which were revolutionary in Montessori's day, have become accepted practice of all good early years provision. It is also recognised that many children of this age benefit from open floor space that can be used for a variety of individual or group activities, as many three and four years olds do not particularly enjoy sitting at a table. Montessori also advocated that the garden has a covered terrace that would give children opportunities to be inside or outside in any weather conditions.

The organisation of the materials, activities and occupations on open shelving according to areas of learning and representing the Montessori early years curriculum (further explained in Chapter 3) is another aspect of the favourable environment that offers availability and accessibility. These materials are usually arranged in a specific order, setting out a possible sequence that the child may or may not choose to adopt. This sequence follows the growing complexity of the activities and the gradual building of specific skills and so scaffolds the child's learning. Each activity is presented on a tray, in a basket or in a box, with all the resources complete and available in a self-contained manner. Once a child selects it from the shelf, they have all the resources necessary for that activity. This completeness provides for focused work, and lack of distraction once the occupation has been chosen. Generally, each activity has its place in the classroom in order to support the child's freedom of choice and the sensitive period for order. This facilitates consistency and predictability within the environment. It is the teacher's role to ensure the consistency and predictability of the environment are maintained.

Freedom of movement and choice

The favourable environment that provides children with a wide range of accessible and available activities designed to meet their individual needs will also facilitate the child's need for freedom. To facilitate this freedom, teachers need to have trust and respect the child as only then will the children truly have freedom of movement and choice, freedoms that go hand in hand. Children can only make appropriate choices if they have the opportunity to move around the classroom and find what they need to satisfy their inner drive, or 'horme'.

The environment needs to be predictable to facilitate the plans and choices made by the child. When children decide to do what they need to do, they are also able to take as much or as little time to do the activity as they choose. Many children will choose to repeat the same task over and over again, either on the same day or on subsequent days. This need for repetition often relates to the child's sensitive periods and is integral to the freedoms offered within Montessori classrooms, as is freedom from interruption. It is considered Inappropriate to disturb a child deep in concentration on a specific self-chosen activity and it is the duty of the teacher to protect this child.

We must not forget that the child who is 'free to do' also needs to be 'free not to do'. There are those children who prefer to learn by watching others. Having the time to sit and watch or contemplate a ray of sunlight reflects our respect for the individual child as much as the freedom to repeat an activity or the freedom to work without interruption does.

Children also have freedom of speech, which relates directly to the sensitive period for language. The child's ability to express and communicate thoughts and ideas is considered to be an essential part of all pre-school provision, bearing in mind the stages of language development. The calm purposeful atmosphere in a Montessori classroom contributes greatly towards children's developing communication skills.

Personal responsibility

However, all the freedoms of the nursery do not mean limitless licence for the child to do as they please. It is generally considered that freedom carries personal responsibility and therefore there are some expectations the teachers have of the children who access the freedoms of the favourable environment. The collective interest of the group must be considered first, so that children will be actively discouraged from any dangerous or hurtful acts that may endanger themselves or others.

The teachers and other children model appropriate and polite behaviour both in communications and when using the activities available in the classroom. Children are expected to return their chosen activities back to the place where they are kept, complete and ready for another person to use, in other words how they found them. This ability to return materials to the shelf may take quite a lot of modelling and consistency of expectation. A patient and creative approach from the teachers alongside the positive example set by older children will be beneficial to the younger children who may initially find it difficult to remember what is expected of them.

It is these responsibilities that also guide the child towards social awareness, the ability to share and what Montessori calls the 'cohesion of the social unit'. Children mature into their social awareness not only through the modelling of adults but also from examples given by the other children in the group.

The favourable environment supports children's individual progress but it does not mean that the social aspects of life are unimportant. For Montessori, the Children's House also meant family groupings of children, allowing the older, more settled children to model behaviour. They also have the opportunity to become 'teachers' when the younger child needs help or wants to know how to work with a piece of material already familiar to the older child, providing wonderful opportunities for a gentle nurturing of a sense of responsibility in the older children. These children are often the first ones to remind the younger ones to put away their work, or help them with putting on their shoes.

In the Montessori classroom we witness many displays of attentive empathy as well as giving the younger children time to try things on their own. This peer support spontaneously emerges and is seldom prompted by the adults in the classroom. From the point of view of the younger child it seems so much more sensible to be able to follow the lead of a peer whom you admire rather than be guided by the teacher. It is quite common for the older children to share activities with the younger ones and to help them where appropriate. From this spontaneous support for one another grows a unity of the group, which heightens awareness of courteous behaviour, kindness and generosity among the group. 'This unity born among the child, which is produced by a spontaneous need directed by an unconscious power, and vitalized by a social spirit, is a phenomenon needing a name, and I call it "cohesion of the social unit"' (Montessori, 1988a [1949]:212).

Reality and nature

It is imperative that the materials available on the shelf reflect the children's growing developmental needs as well as their interests, and are real or three-dimensional models rather than two-dimensional pictorial representations. For example, if we speak about shells, plants, skeletons or stethoscopes it is best to have these objects actually present in the classroom to encourage exploration of these objects through the senses and the extension of vocabulary. This approach is advocated by the recently published *First Hand Experience, What Matters to Children* (Rich *et al.*, 2005).

To cite another example, the Montessori materials also include a selection of solid (such as a cube, cone and pyramid) and flat shapes (such as a triangle, square and circle), all made of wood, which the child can explore and use to absorb the properties of these shapes. These materials serve as a springboard for exploration of everyday objects with these properties, both found in the classroom as well as at home and in the wider environment.

As it is the teacher who is the custodian of the environment, they ensure that the classroom reflects nature by finding ways of including fresh flowers in the classroom, by offering opportunities for observation of nature both inside and outside the classroom, and by ensuring that the nature table reflects not only the seasons but also the interest of the children, that it is vibrant and alive and enticing. The nature table should also offer opportunities for children to contribute towards the daily life of the classroom.

Beauty and harmony

Another important feature of the favourable environment is its beauty and harmony. Montessori felt very strongly that the environment has to be pleasing so as to invite the child to activity. She also felt that the materials, activities and occupations should entice the child and, for this reason, all other decorations within the room are kept very simple so as not to distract the child's attention. This simplicity also means that the child is able to act autonomously within the environment, not only choosing activities but also having the ability to wash up after snack time, clean the easel if needed after painting, wipe the table should anything get spilled and so on. The child's ability to contribute towards the care of the environment is seen as one of the contributing factors to freedom with responsibility.

The harmony of the environment is represented by the organisation of the classroom and also by the purposeful quiet atmosphere in which children are engaged in self-chosen activities corresponding to their needs. This is one of the fundamental differences between a Montessori classroom and other early years provision – the calmness of the classroom is often commented upon and teachers are asked how it is possible. It is the self-directed nature of the activities that promotes this harmony: if the children are truly free to choose what they need to do and are not coerced into doing things simply because adults ask them to, it is more likely that they will be satisfied, involved and able to concentrate. Generally the Montessori classroom is a hum of activity, not silent, but not loud and chaotic either, characterised by children engaged in activities working on their own, with a friend or in small groups, depending on their age, interest and abilities.

The beauty of the environment symbolises the teachers' commitment to the respect for the children in their care.

The teachers ensure that materials are kept in excellent condition and that their own behaviour is gracious and polite. In fact, the classroom for three to six year olds should truly be a Casa dei Bambini – Children's House – a place in which children are comfortable, relaxed and feel at home so that they can reveal their true nature.

Outcomes of the favourable environment

Montessori observed children in the classroom working on their own and in small groups, some being quick and others taking time to repeat an activity several times, each following their own rhythm. Bearing in mind that within one classroom there may be three, four and five year olds, we also need to acknowledge that any timetable for the morning would be inappropriate because it would disturb the natural rhythms. The span of the morning, usually a three-hour period, is what Montessori termed the work cycle.

During this time children will engage in a variety of activities, and if this period is not interrupted by an adult-imposed timetable, the child will have time to reveal their natural tendencies and sensitive periods. It is wonderful to observe settled children entering the Montessori classroom in the morning. As soon as they have got themselves ready for the day and said goodbye to their parents and carers, they select their piece of work. For some this first piece of work is always the same; it may be painting, a puzzle, a book or a writing task. It may be that way for a week, two, perhaps a month and then it changes, reflecting the child's growing interests and developing sensitive periods. Usually this activity helps them settle into the day.

The child then proceeds to select other activities, each following the same pattern – making a conscious choice, taking the activity to a chosen place, working with it, putting it back into its container, and replacing it on the shelf. This we call the cycle of activity. Within any morning the child will conduct many cycles of activity and will do some of them on their own, others with friends and others with the adults in the environment. As the morning progresses the child usually gets involved in one or two activities that will particularly engage their concentration, and then there will be times when the child begins to wander, finding it more difficult to make a choice.

Montessori (1991 [1918]) believed it was important to give the child the time to find what they need. She warned adults against interrupting the child during the false fatigue (the time of search for the next activity), the child needs to be able to select the subsequent activity by themselves in order to be able to engage in an activity that meets their individual needs, to help them become involved and engaged in what they are doing. Montessori (1988a [1949]) speaks of the child using their volition. These periods of concentrated work interspersed with times of searching are termed by Montessori the curve of work and careful observations of each child should produce evidence of a particular curve of work unique to the individual. The more focused and settled the child is, the longer the periods of engagement are and the shorter the false fatigue is. Montessori warns teachers against stepping in and interrupting the false fatigue as this undermines the child's volition. The teacher who is afraid of losing control of the class replaces the children's will with their own decision to do something with a group or suggests having a snack or going outside, so imposing their own timetable on the rhythm of the individual children.

The child who benefits from the extended work cycle and the freedom within the limits of the favourable environment will gradually be able to exercise a certain amount of self-control. First by putting an activity away, then by thinking of others as they clean the snack table ready for them to use, and finally by having sufficient self-control to be able to share a game with a child, or be able to say 'You have it now, I am happy to wait.' This process of maturation takes time and could be compared to a walk in the mountains, up and down, with some days being easier than others. Gradually over a period of time the child develops self-discipline, having experienced the richness of the environment, compassion, generosity, trust and respect of the teacher, having had the time and the opportunities to know themselves. It is the child with these characteristics whom Montessori calls the normalised child. She used this term, with its admittedly problematic connotation in today's usage, to describe a child who follows the normal/natural path of development, a child who has developed physically, who has had the opportunity to develop their personality and who has also experienced the benefits of being part of a social group.

The teacher

The learning materials developed by Montessori represent the foundation of the prepared environment; however, it is the teacher's duty, based on their observations of individual children, to add, complement or develop these materials to meet the individual's needs. It is incredible that these materials, developed almost one hundred years ago, remain relevant and engaging for children today. However, they must not be seen as the only requirements of the classroom; just as Montessori modified and continuously developed the activities offered to the children of her day, so the Montessori teachers of today have a duty to extend the range of materials on offer. These additions should reflect and complement the principles on which the original materials were developed. This requires well-informed practitioners who have a sound understanding of not only the materials but also of child development, both from the Montessori perspective as well as from the point of view of current developmental theory.

It is also expected that Montessori teachers reflect upon their work with children and are able to share their thoughts and understanding of children with their colleagues and parents. It is my understanding that this reflective practice is an aspect of what Montessori herself called the spiritual preparation of the teacher.

All children have potential, curiosity and interest in engaging in social interaction, establishing relationships, constructing their learning, and engaging with everything the environment brings to them. Teachers are deeply aware of the children's potentials and ensure the environment responds to the children's needs and interests.

When considering the normalised child we must also consider the role of the teacher as a key factor in preparation and maintenance of this favourable environment and so indirectly helping the child follow their natural path of development. Throughout this chapter I have already referred to aspects of the teacher's role in the context of the classroom and I will now reflect on the unique nature of the teacher as a facilitator of the child's learning.

Montessori saw the teacher as the one who manages and oversees the classroom in order for the child to be able to learn spontaneously. While Montessori may have had this focus in mind, it is also evident that many Montessori teachers see their role today as facilitators; they guide and help children's access to the classroom recourses. This is where the teacher makes the link between the environment and its materials and the child. This link is understood to be an active one in terms of the preparation and accessibility of the classroom but a passive one in terms of the conventional teaching role.

Montessori saw the child and their spontaneous interest in the environment as the key to the learning process; therefore she speaks of the child's auto-education or the child's ability to teach themselves through the carefully prepared environment. This approach requires a change in the attitudes of the adults who work with small children.

First and foremost it requires implicit trust in the child's ability to select activities relevant to their stage of development and also trust and understanding of the materials available to the child. The teacher must be confident in knowing that whatever is on offer in the classroom has a specific purpose that will benefit the child in some aspect of their development.

It also requires an adult who will be able to help the children settle into the environment, to show them how it works and what it has to offer and then to withdraw when the child is able to access the activities on their own. This approach gives children the opportunity to observe, explore and investigate the environment. This does not mean that the teacher abandons the child; they continue to observe and will lend a hand should the child need it, possibly suggesting a different approach or asking another child to offer help. The teacher may also join the child once an activity has been completed so that they can talk about what the child discovered or why they approached the problem in a certain way, or admire the outcome. However, Montessori warns us about interruption of the child who is concentrating on a task, as this interruption may disturb a train of thought or the moment when a problem is just about to be solved. Montessori sees this interruption as undermining the child's efforts. The teacher's role changes from an active one to that of a more passive facilitator. This is referred to by Standing (1984:302–304), rather confusingly, as 'transference of activity'. The teacher continues to modify the environment for individual children through observation and occasional lessons. The lessons are offered when the child is ready to be introduced to new areas of the classroom or aspects of their learning.

This change of role is the biggest challenge for the Montessori teacher; at any one time there are children in the classroom who require more active interactions, while some will be less dependent and others will themselves become the teachers of the younger children. This is where the teacher's ability to observe, reflect upon and interpret children's behaviour will be their most useful tools. These observations will also serve as a means of record keeping and assessment and to inform any planning and modification of the environment.

Many adults are attracted to Montessori teaching by her vision of the child as an autonomous learner and our own desire to share what we know with children. It is inevitable that these two aspects of our motivation will be in conflict with each other and how each one of us resolves this conflict results in the quality of Montessori provision for the children in our care.

The preparation of the teacher that Montessori talks about in her writings (1964 [1912], 1966 and 1988a [1949]) requires sound knowledge of the Montessori philosophy as well as pedagogy, incorporating aspects of these two disciplines to develop observational skills and teaching strategies, as well as knowledge and understanding of how children develop and learn. Inevitably the teachers of today, and of the future, will also need to know about the current legislation and requirements for caring for young children, as well as being familiar with the current trends in early years education and care. Like all teachers, the Montessori teacher will have to be committed to continued learning, as teaching is also a process of learning.

Montessori herself did not envisage that the Montessori teachers of the future would be some all-knowing individuals. Instead she wanted them to be humble and open, respecting the child as a human being filled with potential.

Chapter 3

The Montessori early years curriculum

Learning is holistic

Montessori saw education as a key to child development and a main contributing factor to the child's preparation for life. However, she also recognised that young children do not learn subjects, but that their learning is holistic in its nature. The child's ability to observe, explore, investigate, ask questions and so to learn about their environment is not necessarily organised into lessons or subjects. The child observes and explores when they become interested.

This child needs an adult who is able to respond to their investigations wherever and whenever they occur – whether in the bath, while listening to a story, on a walk, when digging in the garden or during a lesson. A responsive adult will be able to answer, question, wonder or observe with the child and together they may discover some of the answers. It is also possible that the child will need adults who listen to their hypotheses, discoveries and investigations and simply smile or nod in response.

Therefore if we wish to define the early years curriculum we need to recognise that in the early years 'learning occurs constantly whether intentionally or incidentally' (MacLeod-Brunell, 2004:45). We need to examine not only what the child learns but also how, in order to appreciate the complexities of learning in the early years.

Play is the best tool for learning

It is also generally agreed today that play is the most effective tool for the child's learning (Bruce, 1991; Jenkinson, 2002; Moyles, 2005). Here we have to try to unravel one of the big Montessori conundrums: early on, in the first Children's House, Montessori discovered that children preferred work to play, and so throughout her writings she refers to children working, rather than playing.

This emphasis on work as opposed to play has constituted one of the key criticisms of the Montessori legacy by the early years community. It is important to try to understand what Montessori herself meant. Her observations of children led her to the understanding that the nature of the child's work is fundamentally different to the nature of the adult's work. According to Montessori, the child is interested in the process whereas the adult is interested in the product. The child is happy to repeat the process; they are perfecting their skills through the repetition. Just think of a three year old who is helping to wash up, standing at the sink and washing the same plate over and over again: they wash it, put it on the draining board and then take it back off and wash it again. The repetition serves as a tool of self-construction, and in turn of the construction of the human being.

'A child is also a worker and producer. Although he cannot share in the work of adults, he has his own difficult and important task to perform, that of producing a man' (Montessori, 1966:193). This quotation reflects another perspective on the work versus play debate; Montessori recognised the enormous task all children undertake within the developmental process of

Figure 3.1 Doctor's surgery

growing up and maturing. She saw this to be the child's work. According to Montessori, all the activities within the classroom contribute to the child's development. So, when children engage in these activities they are working towards 'the creation/construction of man'.

This philosophical perspective on the nature of the growing child should be considered every time Montessori speaks in earnest of the child's work. I believe Montessori's emphasis on work needs to be seen as the child's need to do, to be active, to manipulate and so to learn – it does not negate the importance of play.

We also need to consider the historical perspective of Montessori's writing. Her discoveries, on which the majority of her writing is based, were made in the early twentieth century. At this time there was little psychological knowledge about children; Montessori's ideas were formulated before Melanie Klein and Anna Freud developed their thoughts about play therapy, before A.S. Neil set up the Summerhill school, or John Holt (1967) wrote *How Children Learn*. Montessori's own life bears testimony to the importance of diligence and hard work if we want to achieve anything as individuals; therefore, it is not surprising that she focuses so much on work and the task of self-construction.

It is also important to highlight that many of today's Montessori practitioners would acknowledge the importance of play in the lives of children. The present-day training of Montessori teachers explores the issues relating to the nature of the child's work and play. Children themselves relate to work in their play such as when pretending to be their parents or when they come to early years settings ready to do 'work'.

In the context of the Montessori classroom, it is up to us as practitioners not to differentiate between play and work, just as the child does not – they are simply keen to do things! Yet how often has one heard: 'You can do the blocks after you have done some numbers with me'? The mathematical learning offered by the blocks is potentially wider, contextually more appropriate as well as far more enjoyable for the child – but it needs a sensitive adult to make links, explain or listen to what the child has to say about their learning.

Montessori areas of learning

Whether we call it work or play, the activities in the Montessori classroom have clearly defined aims and so contribute to the child's development as well as to the content of the child's learning; they represent the curriculum. This curriculum is led by the needs of the individual (MacLeod-Brudenell, 2004).

As mentioned in Chapter 2 in the discussion about the favourable environment in which the child learns, the Montessori areas of learning broadly correspond with the physical organisation of the classroom. In most Montessori classrooms for three to six year olds you will find activities for the following:

■ practical life (or daily living);

■ refinement of the senses;

■ communication, language and literacy;

■ mathematics;

■ cultural aspects of life (or 'knowledge and understanding of the world' in the foundation stage curriculum);

■ creativity.

Practical life

The activities in this area reflect the children's need to model behaviours on their parents and their family life. They also allow children to contribute towards the cultural and social life of the classroom, offering them the opportunity to feel a sense of belonging.

The main aim of the practical life exercises is to make a link between the home and the new environment of the Montessori classroom. This is done by representing tasks and activities with which children are already familiar from their home environment such as pouring, dusting, getting dressed, sweeping the classroom or leaves in the garden and so on.

While they are carrying out these activities the children perfect basic skills that will aid their independence both in the classroom as well as at home. They learn to pour their own drinks, serve food, tidy their own work, wash their hands, wash up after their snack, water and tend to the plants in the classroom, feed the pets and many more skills. The main aim of any practical life activity is to develop and perfect certain skills that will contribute towards the child's autonomy.

The other fundamental aspect common to all practical life activities is their active nature. Children manipulate and so perfect their gross and fine

Figure 3.2 Practical life activities ready for use

Figure 3.3 Cleaning utensils

motor skills as well as coordination of movement, eye–hand coordination, dexterity and pincer grip. Just imagine the range of physical skills required to use pegs, scissors, tongs or tweezers, to plant a seed, to rake the lawn or to offer a snack to a friend.

Linked with these specific skills are also general indirect benefits that apply to most practical life activities. Concentration, the need to organise, sequence and order the activity, and attention to detail are all benefits that the practical life curriculum offers to children.

In addition, all the activities involve movement, manipulation and refinement of physical skills; just consider the skills required in sewing with a needle or painting at an easel. Having started with relatively easy activities such as pouring water from a jug into a glass or washing a plate, these activities are then incorporated into the daily life of the classroom.

And of course as mentioned previously, all these attributes contribute to the child's independence. Consider the following example of a two and half/three year old deciding to have a snack. They will know the routine of what is required, for example,

■ first check if there is a space available at the snack table;

■ select from the food on offer such as fruit, raisins, biscuit, cracker or a rice cake;

■ select a drink and pour it into a glass;

■ take the plate with the snack and the glass with the drink to the snack table;

■ eat it while chatting to a friend;

■ when finished wash it all up, dry it; and

■ dry their hands ready to do something else.

This routine illustrates well how self-contained individual practical life activities contribute to the complex routine of having a snack and how much the child learns from every such routine. Physical activity contributes to the holistic development of the child in the following ways:

■ The sequence requires memory, problem solving and estimation when choosing the snack and drink and when washing the dishes.

■ The social interaction at the snack table contributes towards growing social awareness and communication skills. Often two friends will decide to have a snack together and will be helpful to each other as well as have some fun while eating.

■ When all is finished, imagine the sense of achievement for the three year old who has managed it all by themselves, including the washing up!

There are many examples of such complex routines in the Montessori classroom that build on the individual skills practised in the practical life area of the classroom.

Generally the practical life activities are divided into three distinct groups (Gettman, 1987):

■ Exercises for refinement of movement – such as pouring, transferring, cutting, gluing, folding, opening and closing of boxes/bottles, and threading.

■ Exercises for care of the environment – such as sweeping, polishing, dusting.

■ Washing and looking after plants, pets and the garden.

■ Exercises for care of self that include activities and skills supporting personal independence – such as washing hands and blowing one's nose, as well activities promoting grace and courtesy – such as greeting visitors, offering a snack to a friend, and asking for help.

The practical life activities are often the first area of interest for the newcomer to a Montessori classroom because of their familiarity, relative simplicity and self-contained nature. However, as children become more competent, the skills acquired in this area will be used daily in supporting the organisation and maintenance of the classroom. They become the daily life of the classroom as children will offer to wipe tables after an activity, will sweep up after lunch, wash the dishes or dirty polishing cloths. The activities take on social importance and give children opportunities to contribute to the well being of the group, and in the process boost their self-esteem and reflect their responsibilities within the group – a positive illustration of the 'cohesion of the social unit' we have discussed in the previous chapter.

The practical life activities also often act as the 'secure base' (Bowlby, 1988) for children who may be worried or anxious; their simplicity will offer security and predictability as well as opportunities to be successful at achieving the chosen tasks. Whilst children carry on with their practical life activities you will often overhear their monologues reflecting symbolic play

(Piaget, 1962). As they pour water from a jug to a glass, they are preparing a cup of tea for a friend, or medicine for their sick dolly. In this way the activities act as a catalyst for spontaneous imaginative play, which often takes place in the 'home corner' of other nurseries.

It is important to add that just as these activities reflect everyday life, Montessori believed it was very important that they also reflect the culture of the children. Today's Montessori classrooms are often as international as the approach and so you may well observe the use of chopsticks, preparation of Arabic dishes, or re-enactment of a Japanese tea ceremony as well as the use of African beads in threading activities or making of bread for a harvest festival.

As part of this area of learning you may encounter a game called Walking on the Line. Fundamentally, this is a balancing game, focusing on following a line drawn on the floor. It also gives children tasks such as carrying different objects, a flag or a glass with water while they walk on the line. This activity also offers challenges in negotiating if several children take part in the game.

Another game often played in Montessori classrooms is the Silence Game. This game has been inspired by a baby visiting a Montessori classroom. The baby's stillness prompted Montessori to urge the children to listen to the stillness and quietness created not only by everybody's adoration of the baby but also by the baby herself. Montessori developed this exercise further to test the children's hearing and their ability to contribute to a quiet moment shared by the whole group. The Silence Game gives children the opportunity to demonstrate their self-discipline during the shared quiet moment.

Refinement of the senses

Activities in this area of the classroom represent the early materials developed by Montessori. Some of these were inspired by Froebel's Gifts, such as the geometric solids, while others can be linked with Seguin and still others are Montessori's own inventions.

The main purpose of these activities is to help the child organise and classify the impressions of the environment gathered during earlier stages of their life. Sensorial materials offer systematic refinement of the five senses as well as the child's stereognostic and kinaesthetic sense, which represents the exploration of three- and two-dimensional forms (in the Montessori context, the geometric solids such as cubes, prisms, cones, pyramids, and outlines of squares, circles, triangle).

For Montessori these materials hold the key to the understanding of fundamental concepts and the possibility of the expansion of the child's cognitive capabilities. The materials respond to the child's sensitive period for refinement of the senses, offer opportunities for manipulation and the extension of vocabulary. With their frequent focus on matching, pairing, sorting and grading they are also integral to building the foundation for mathematical understanding (Liebeck, 1984).

Figure 3.4 Exploring textures

Figure 3.5 Sensorial activities and unit blocks ready for use

The activities for the refinement of the senses focus the child's attention and learning on each of their different senses:

■ The visual sense: the child explores the properties and relationship of cubes, prisms, cylinders and rods, as well as the relationship of colours and their shades.

■ The stereognostic sense: the child builds on the visual experiences of geometric forms as they explore the properties of the solid shapes by grouping them according to same/similar properties (such as whether or not a shape rolls), comparing them to the two-dimensional shapes of their bases and matching pairs of solid shapes. An activity in this area, which focuses on the tactile aspects, without using visual discrimination, is the mystery bag. This bag contains sets of matching objects; the child is expected to pair them by feel. The child also has an opportunity to learn about flat shapes using both the visual and kinaesthetic senses. They explore them further as they come to work with the binomial and trinomial cubes. The knowledge of flat shapes is extended by giving children opportunities to make patterns.

■ The tactile sense: the child explores varying textures of sandpapers, fabrics and papers. The child also has the opportunity to work with tablets of varying weight and temperature.

■ The auditory sense: the child engages in a range of activities that heighten listening skills using sound boxes. In addition the child is introduced to the basics of musical notation using the bells.

■ Taste and smell: the child does activities involving food, including cooking, and learns about flowers, fruits and vegetables in cultural lessons.

The activities available in the sensorial area offer children keys to the universe – points of reference to key concepts such as shape, size and so on. They are organised in such a way as to support assimilation and accommodation of schemas and so contribute towards concept formation through the manipulative nature of the activities. For Montessori vocabulary expansion has a specific purpose in the context of these materials and in order to teach new vocabulary the Montessori teacher uses a technique developed by Seguin called the three-period lesson.

The sequence in which we work with the sensorial materials focuses first on exploration of qualities, then on systematic identification of properties of the materials followed by vocabulary expansion that serves to 'polarise the child's attention', as Montesorri called it, and so to maximise the child's learning potential.

From the point of view of Montessori education today, the sensorial activities still form the foundation of later academic learning. It is also important to understand that like all foundations, the opportunity to extend the child's knowledge of these concepts and apply them to contexts that are familiar and meaningful to the child is very important. Through the application of these concepts in social context we can see what the children learned and understood by using the sensorial materials. For example, it is important for Montessori teachers to offer opportunities for open-ended exploration of the qualities and properties of shapes by offering children opportunities to use unit blocks (Gura, 1992). They can also make patterns using collage and drawing, or, for the older child, extend their knowledge of the Montessori bells and music notation to playing an instrument or being encouraged to compose original music.

We can also encourage immediate extensions of classroom learning into the outdoor environment by applying the tactile classroom experiences to finding rough and smooth surfaces in the garden or on a nature walk.

Equally outdoor experiences can be applied to activities available inside the classroom such a looking up a bug in a book or playing sound lotto, which relates to sounds from nature such as bird song or thunder.

Sensorial activities prepare children for other areas of learning. It has been pointed out that by working with the geometric forms and other materials the child learns to classify and organise information by matching, pairing and grading objects; this will be beneficial when exploring the one-to-one correspondence between quantities and symbols in mathematics, and when sequencing numerals. Many of the sensorial activities will also serve as beneficial preparation for other areas of learning, such as listening for small differentiations in sounds, which will tune the ear to listening out for letter sounds. The child will use visual, auditory and tactile experiences when they are introduced to sandpaper letters or numerals (as described on pp. 35 and 36), when letter/numeral shapes will be absorbed kinaesthetically, using all three senses as well as muscular memory.

Communication, language and literacy

Montessori was surprised by children's ability to learn to write and read much earlier than generally expected when she started to explore the possibilities in this area of learning. This was at the request of the parents whose children attended the first Children's House. It is important to understand and appreciate that introducing reading and writing in the Montessori classroom is possible because of the foundation laid in the practical life and sensorial areas of the classroom.

In addition the availability of books, the increased phonological awareness of the child (achieved through games such as Odd Man Out or simplified I Spy) play a crucial role in laying the foundation for learning to write and read. However it is also important to remember that not all children will be ready or interested in being introduced to letters and writing at the age of three or four; the key to identifying the child's readiness remains in the adult's observations and conversations with the child.

The journey towards reading and writing is often initially motivated by personal interest, such as recognition of one's own, a friend's or sibling's names. It is vital that we acknowledge that in the early years this journey is likely to be longer and not as clearly defined as it is when the child is five, six or seven.

Ever since the early days, Montessorians have approached this area of learning through phonics, focusing on letter sounds and shapes using the

Figure 3.6 Story time outside

sandpaper letters. They provide a multi-sensory approach to absorption of the letter sounds as well as shapes by both visual and tactile means.

Children are prepared for use of writing implements early both through the refinement of their fine motor movements within the practical life areas of the classroom and within the creative area. Their ability to control a pencil is further refined by the use of insets for design.

The child first learns to build words using cut-out letters (as many children do at home using magnetic letters to form their names and words on the fridge) and by careful listening to letter sounds. They start by building words with predictable patterns of a single, short vowel placed between the two consonants, such as cat and mat. Use of 'onset and rime' (Lawrence, 1998; MCI, 2006) at this stage of learning serves as an important tool for the introduction of reading and so the decoding of words.

Further challenges are presented by consonant blends such as pr- (pram), fr- (frog) and st- (stem, stamp). They are introduced before words with more complex spelling are tackled by focusing on a specific sound and (one of) its corresponding spelling(s), such as the a-e sound in plate.

The child has the opportunity to work systematically through boxes identifying blends, diagraph, trigraphs and phonograms. The box activities focus on reading, while word-building activities highlight spelling patterns for the children. Further reading opportunities are offered by word lists, phrase and sentence strips and reading books accompanying the different levels of complexity required in reading.

In the Montessori classroom, children are also introduced to grammar using colour coding for parts of speech and building sentences with the help of objects. These activities offer a sensorial introduction to grammar and also serve as reading tools.

Wherever possible we offer the child objects that can be manipulated in order to both prompt and scaffold the child's learning. In Britain today, most children leave the Montessori classroom soon after they are four years of age. It is the phonological awareness and general pre-reading activities such as storytelling, using books with props or sequencing of stories that prepare children for more systematic literacy work in primary schools.

Mathematics

The child is introduced to pre-maths concepts such as matching and sorting as well as to geometry within the sensorial area of the classroom. Children often come to nursery with passive knowledge of numbers through everyday use, such as counting steps, reciting nursery rhymes and looking at number books. They may also have the ability, for example, to count the three candles on a birthday cake and recognise the numeral on a birthday card.

The Montessori maths materials offer a systematic approach to learning about the integrity of numbers in relation to numerals, always using manipulatives and objects to support the learning. The golden bead materials, designed to introduce children to the hierarchies of the decimal system while exploring the place value using both the beads and the written symbols of the large number cards, is probably the most unique and original contribution made by Montessori to the learning of mathematics. They give the child the opportunity to explore the relationships between the hierarchies of the decimal system before the child is presented with addition and subtraction of units.

All activities within the nursery mathematics syllabus are presented to the child through the use of objects while gradually building an understanding of number and memorising the processes of addition, subtraction, multiplication and division.

Figure 3.7 Organising geometric shapes particular to individual children in the group

Figure 3.8 Exploring fractions

Montessori classrooms also give children opportunities to use number knowledge in everyday contexts and within contexts meaningful to the child, such as counting how many biscuits will be needed for snack or recognising numerals on a birthday chart. Number books are available and children often play number games in the garden or playground, while cooking and gardening, and these serve as meaningful tools for the application of counting skills in the daily life of the classroom.

Cultural aspects of life

This area of the classroom has the least prescribed materials. It offers opportunities for children and teachers to explore a wide range of topics of interest in biology, geography and history. The activities in this area should centre on real experiences that give children opportunities to observe, explore and investigate such things as trees, seasons, farmyard animals, the solar system, how a volcano works and so on.

In the areas of natural sciences such as botany and zoology we start by observing and becoming familiar with the immediate environment within the child's community. We work from the opposite perspective in geography, embracing the whole solar system and explore the natural

Figure 3.9 Engaged with the farm

Figure 3.10 Summer lunchtime

aspects of global physical geography before looking at the continents and countries where we live.

The nature table is often used as the focus for this area of learning. A range of teacher-made materials complement the child's initial real experiences. These materials support and develop the child's language and literacy skills and encourage the child's individual learning by using primarily matching and pairing teaching strategies.

Like most of the materials in the Montessori classroom these ones are designed to be used by individual children or small groups, supported when necessary by an adult. Very few of these materials are suitable for large group teaching. Most of the activities in this area of learning should be planned with the children and built on their interest, rather than determined by adult perceptions of what the child should learn.

History is explored through time lines and natural cycles that help children understand the passage of time, a concept alien to most children. This is seen as preparation for a more systematic study of natural history from an evolutionary perspective.

The exploration of continents and their countries also gives us opportunities to explore similarities and differences in the lives of children and their families around the world. Montessori saw these activities as important learning tools in developing children's understanding of and respect for all humanity as a foundation towards peaceful co-existence. Peace education continues to be a key aspect of the spiritual development of the child in the Montessori classroom and is extensively enlarged upon in the Montessori primary curriculum through the concept of cosmic education.

For Montessori cosmic education represents not only the idea that each one of us is part of the larger cosmos but also that we are in a state of constant change or evolution. Nothing is static in the universe, and all living as well as not living aspects of our existence are interconnected and interdependent on each other. This inter-relationship places a great responsibility on each one of us. We are all part of this universal link and our individual actions and behaviours ultimately impact on the existence of all humanity.

Figure 3.11 Learning outside

Creativity

This area of the Montessori classroom acknowledges the importance of self-expression and highlights the need for children to have opportunities to participate in self-chosen and self-initiated arts and craft activities, as well as music and movement and socio-dramatic play.

A well-equipped Montessori nursery has an area of the classroom where children have all the necessary resources freely available to paint, using both an easel and watercolours. Children are also given the opportunity to draw using a range of good quality tools such a crayons, coloured pencils

Figure 3.12 Building with unit blocks

and felt tips as well as a variety of different kinds of paper. They also have resources to glue and make collages, and to print using stamps as well as natural resources such as vegetables, wood or sponge stamps. Teachers help children to develop skills necessary for the activities, such as how to apply glue or use scissors, but the activities themselves are open-ended and offer endless possibilities for self-expression.

Musical instruments, particularly percussion instruments, are also available for spontaneous use, and teachers sing regularly with the children. Specialist music teachers may come to sing or do music and movement activities.

Storytelling, as well as story time using books and props, is commonplace in Montessori classrooms. This often happens spontaneously when a child asks for a story, and usually a small group gathers around the adult in the book area of the classroom. Some nurseries also have story time for the whole group at the end of the day. All these activities can be incorporated into the spontaneous, choice-led work cycle and do not require all children to stop what they are doing in order to participate.

Many of these activities happen inside the classroom but there are also opportunities for these activities to be conducted outside the classroom. You may also see a Montessori teacher dramatising stories for children to act out. What you may not see is a role play area using a wide range of props that has been set up by adults on a particular theme, such as a shop or a post office. Much of the role play in Montessori classrooms is spontaneous, inspired by clothes from around the world or emerging from the variety of topics studied in the classroom, such as visits to the seaside or the zoo, or as previously mentioned emerging from work in the practical life area of the classroom.

Chapter 4
Montessori and the foundation stage

The aim of the Montessori curriculum

In the previous chapters we have discussed what is understood today by Montessori education. It was Montessori's aim and it remains the aim of today's Montessori practitioners to provide young children with a wide range of experiences in support of spontaneous development of the whole child. The focus is on the child's growing manipulative skills and concentration, which result in independence. With growing independence the child is able to use their initiative and meet new challenges.

All this is achieved in a calm atmosphere conducive to learning. As a result, the majority of children leave Montessori classrooms with enthusiasm for learning, autonomy and ability to embrace risks. Their social skills help them to negotiate their learning both with peers and adults. In short they are ready to meet the challenges of the new learning environment, be it in the maintained or independent sector.

The foundation stage curriculum

Since the early 1990s we have witnessed an increased interest in early years education from the government. This has resulted in greater awareness of parents in what pre-school education has to offer their children. It is inevitable that, as government funding has become available for the education of the very young, guidance for delivery of an appropriate and relevant educational framework would be developed.

This framework is outlined in the Curriculum Guidance for the Foundation Stage. It offers early years practitioners in England a guidance on how to introduce young children to learning and how to meet the learning goals set out in the six areas of learning that are represented in this curriculum.

Within each area of learning the document identifies stepping stones, guiding the practitioner through aspects of learning and towards the achievement of the early learning goals by the time the child completes the reception year.

This is fundamentally a product-led curriculum (Kelly, 1989), which embraces the developmental nature of early years learning. We can see the developmental aspect in the titles that were selected for the areas of learning, such as personal, social and emotional development, physical and creative development. The process of how the child achieves the individual goals remains at the discretion of the practitioner or setting, but over the years the stepping stones in the early learning goals have been embedded into early years practice and have become part of the process.

Links between Montessori individual learning plans and the early learning goals

The Montessori learning materials, their organisation and availability within the Montessori classroom and the way that Montessori practitioners introduce them to children form part of the learning process and so represent the Montessori early years curriculum. They also provide a framework for learning and are outlined in the record cards that Montessori nurseries keep for individual children. Furthermore they are organised in a sequential manner and are usually used as planning tools.

Many schools have renamed their records cards individual learning plans as each activity on the plan has clearly stated aims within the Montessori schemes of work. These schemes of work are contained within Montessori files, or albums; each student has to prepare them as part of their training. Each activity has a clearly defined aim and process as well as progression. In this way the 'Montessori classroom becomes the curriculum'.

With the introduction of the foundation stage curriculum Montessori practitioners had to make links between early learning goals and the activities offered in Montessori classrooms, explaining the progression and differentiation built into the materials.

While all Montessori teachers and practitioners share in the Montessori legacy, how the legacy is interpreted will vary from nursery to nursery. The range of materials on offer will also vary depending on the individual schools, with some nurseries offering the full range of Montessori equipment while others adding and supplementing it with contemporary learning materials in keeping within the Montessori methodology – such as the unit blocks.

It became imperative for each setting to explain these links and therefore the Montessori early years curriculum has been mapped against the foundation stage curriculum. (For the specific links between Montessori practice and the early learning goals in the foundation stage curriculum, see Appendix 1, p. 56.)

Montessori training colleges offer continued professional development relating to the foundation stage curriculum and its relevance to Montessori practice. There is also a comprehensive computerised programme, which provides a record-keeping facility for technologically minded Montessorians.

Links between the Montessori early years curriculum and the foundation stage

The principles of the foundation stage curriculum can be summarised as follows:

- practitioners should ensure that all children feel included, secure and valued;
- no child should be excluded or disadvantaged;
- early years experiences should build on what children already know and can do;
- parents and practitioners should work together;
- the early years curriculum should be carefully structured;
- there should be opportunities for children to engage in activities planned by adults and also those that they plan or initiate themselves;
- practitioners must be able to observe and respond appropriately to children;
- well-planned, purposeful activity and appropriate intervention by practitioners will engage children in the learning process;
- the learning environment should be well planned and organised;
- care and education must be of high quality.

Many aspects of these principles resonate comfortably with Montessori principles, summarised here:

- pedagogy is embedded in the developmental needs of the child;

- the settling in process and how the child feels about coming to nursery will affect all their learning;

- each child comes to the nursery with unique potential and abilities and it is then the role of the teacher to build on and develop them;

- parents are the child's first educators and can influence and contribute to nursery life; there must be mutual understanding and respect between the nursery and children's families;

- the curriculum is holistic and recognises that learning is integrated and developmental;

- activities are organised in the prepared environment and available to the children;

- there are opportunities for both adult-led and spontaneously chosen activities;

- classroom planning is based on observations of individual children and responds to their developmental needs and interests;

- practitioners offer high-quality learning;

- learning and teaching go hand in hand, and teachers respond to the needs of individual children.

Montessori recognised early in her career that learning is inseparable from life and young children's development. Children's ability to absorb and organise stimuli received from contact with their environment and from interaction with peers, parents and carers means that children learn from birth. This feature of learning is now acknowledged by the majority of early years educators.

What makes the Montessori approach unique is her deep belief in the child's self-construction and the role of the adult as a supporter and facilitator of this process. These ideals underpin the fundamental principles of the Montessori philosophy.

Organisation of the Montessori early years curriculum into the six areas of learning

Montessori was one of the first early years educators to develop a structured approach to learning, an approach that generally begins with the child being introduced to practical life and sensorial education. These two areas of learning serve as the foundation for later work in mathematics and literacy. Cultural and creative activities are also part of daily life in Montessori classrooms and complement, link and extend what children are learning in the other areas.

Children's learning in the early years is not compartmentalised and areas of learning are closely connected and linked. This is particularly so because children learn by doing. Manipulative skills and refinement of coordination of movement feature in every area of learning.

The Montessori areas of learning can be organised into the six areas of learning identified by the foundation stage curriculum.

- personal, social and emotional development;
- communication, language and literacy;
- mathematical development;
- knowledge and understanding of the world;
- physical development;
- creative development.

Personal, social and emotional development

When exploring the aspects of this area of learning we find that the ground rules as well as the opportunities to work with the activities for an extended period of time support children's dispositions. The teachers and older children model attitudes of kindness, politeness as well as perseverance and diligence.

Self-confidence and self-esteem are nurtured by the independence gained from perfecting skills such as pouring, transferring, learning to do buttons and buckles, helping look after animals and plants in the classroom and in the garden. As children grow more competent in what they do they are able to support every aspect of daily routine in the classroom, sometimes on their own and other times with the help of friends and adults.

This participation contributes towards establishing relationships with their teachers. Peer friendships and cooperation are extended as children settle into the classroom and learn to take turns by returning materials back to the shelves, or share in activities such as preparation for lunch, or gardening.

Ground rules as well as role models provided by the teachers and older children encourage positive behaviour and self-control grows out of the freedoms offered by the classroom and the responsibility that comes with the freedom – such as being able to choose what to do but knowing that the activity has to be returned back to the shelf, ready for another child to use. Courteous behaviour is modelled and encouraged at all times.

The practical life area is organised into three groups, and the area for 'care of self' where children learn to wash their hands, put on shoes and clothes when going outside or returning home or brushing their teeth after meals contributes directly to the self-care aspect of this area of learning.

The fact that the child is able to contribute towards the daily organisation and routines of classroom life makes a major contribution to their sense of belonging and therefore sense of community. Through celebrations of festivals and culturally appropriate practical life activities, such as learning to put on a kimono, setting table for Chinese lunch or giving thanks at harvest festival, children extend their sense of community beyond the boundaries of their immediate and familiar environment.

Communication, language and literacy

In this area of learning there are six key aspects, which focus on communication as well as use of language as a cognitive skill and the introduction of reading and writing.

Montessori wrote extensively in *The Absorbent Mind* of the importance of language development and the role adults play in developing communications skills. The Montessori classroom encourages conversation, discussion and dialogue as part of the everyday life of the classroom. Language for communication is evident in every aspect of learning – during group time, in small group activities when games are played or science experiments carried out, when children work in pairs or alone and when monologues are often overheard as children talk themselves through what they are doing.

Language for thinking is encouraged by extending children's vocabulary through three-period lessons so ensuring that children have the opportunities to express themselves using appropriate language. Children are also encouraged to talk about their work and ask questions to help them in problem solving and exploration of materials. Storybooks play an important role in extending children's communication skills by offering rich and imaginative use of language. Information books support children's thinking and memory.

Montessori teachers approach reading and writing simultaneously and base their lessons on the phonic approach. The multi-sensory benefits of the sandpaper letters give children opportunities to be introduced both to the letter shape and sound as children hear the sound of the individual letters while they trace their shape outlined in sandpaper. There can be no more effective way of linking the two together.

However, much work has to be done in order to develop children's phonic awareness prior to introducing the sandpaper letters. Games such as I Spy and Odd Man Out contribute greatly to children's awareness of letter sounds and give them the opportunity to link letter sound with initial sounds in their names and in words. Rhymes, poems and stories further contribute towards the child's awareness of letters and their sounds.

Letter shapes and sounds are introduced simultaneously and children are prepared for writing long before we introduce them to the insets for design, the materials specifically developed by Montessori to help control of pencil, lightness of touch and directionality of writing. The majority of practical life and sensorial exercises develop manipulative skills and focus on the dynamic tripod grip and develop the hand muscles and flexible wrist in preparation for holding a pencil.

In addition, children in Montessori classrooms benefit from easily accessible writing implements that are usually available alongside the inset for design or in the art area of the classroom. Accessibility of painting at an easel cannot be underestimated as an important contribution to the development of arm movement and gross motor skills required prior to developing the smaller muscles supporting the use of writing implements. Children are also encouraged to 'write without writing' using their knowledge of letter sounds and letter shapes to formulate words with the Large Movable Alphabet.

As awareness has grown in the importance of cursive letter shapes, many Montessori nursery schools have been using the Sasoon Cursive Alphabet for their sandpaper letters so encouraging appropriate letter formation and focusing on the exit strokes used in joined-up handwriting. This gives children an excellent preparation for the more formal lessons in handwriting that they will receive in primary schools.

Reading is introduced in a three-tier approach, focusing on three-letter words consisting of 'consonant, vowel, consonant' words such as 'cat' at the beginning level. Children utilise their knowledge of letters and are prepared for blending of sounds into words by word building and 'onset and rime' activities.

Initially children 'read words' and use objects to match to word cards they have read. Gradually, as they get more practice decoding words, they use fewer props and move from single words to reading phrases, sentences and books.

The same progression is followed at the second level when children tackle initial and final blends such as pr- in pram or -lt in kilt. Double consonant, as in carrot or bonnet, and -ck are introduced next, and most common digraphs such as sh- in shell, ch- in chips and th- in thin feature next.

These prepare children for the third stage of reading, when individual phonograms are studied, first by reading and then by focusing on the spelling patterns in words like barn (b-ar-n). Before children progress onto the third reading level, they also study grammar and colour coding is used to introduce parts of speech.

These early grammar activities not only introduce parts of speech but also give children the opportunity to practise their reading. Unfortunately as most children in England leave Montessori nursery schools around the age of four, they seldom benefit from the full range of reading activities available to children in the United States or in Europe who usually attend Montessori schools until the age of six.

Mathematical development

The preparation for mathematics that children receive in Montessori schools starts in the sensorial area as children refine their senses by exploring shape, pattern and weight. These activities introduce concepts of one-to-one correspondence (knobbed cylinders), seriation (the pink tower, the broad stair, long rods and coloured cylinders), sorting (constructive triangles) and so on.

Mathematical concepts are experienced and absorbed by children long before they are introduced to mathematics in a formal way. This is one of the reasons why Montessori refers to the sensorial materials as 'materialised abstractions'. Children in Montessori classrooms have the opportunity to be introduced to mathematical language in context of everyday life of the classroom, such as during register time, having snacks, during cooking sessions, in the art and book areas.

The Montessori mathematical curriculum focuses primarily on number and the relationships between quantities and written symbols. A range of materials help children understand the unique relationship between numbers as labels and for counting. The materials highlight the one-to-one correspondence between quantity and symbol as children use number rods and cards, the spindle box, and cards and counters. This foundation to the number base of ten is further explored when children are introduced to the hierarchies of the decimal system. They use the golden bead material and colour coded numeral cards and materials for counting up to 100. The patterns created by table exercises are explored by the older children, as are fractions.

Once children have secure knowledge of numbers to ten, they will be also introduced to number operations using a range of activities, such as the group operations with the golden beads, the Snake Game, number rods, short bead stair and strip boards. Calculating using objects and gradually recording the answers is a natural progression from the activities for counting to ten. It also complements the spontaneous calculaton opportunities present in the everyday life of the classroom – during cooking, when using play dough and when working with the sensorial materials and unit blocks.

The sensorial area of learning provides many opportunities for exploration of shape and space. Children use the geometric solids, and their three-dimensional qualities, and the geometric cabinet to become familiar with flat shapes. Gradually they become aware of the relationship between the solid and flat shapes. Naming shapes such as prisms, cuboids, cylinders, pyramids, rectangles, hexagons and parallelograms become part of everyday life of the classroom. The flat and solid shapes give many opportunities to explore spatial relationships and patterns.

Measurement is primarily introduced during cooking activities. We also use the longest (1 metre/100 centimetres) or shortest (10 centimetres) red rods from the sensorial area as a unit of measurement, particularly when considering height and length.

Knowledge and understanding of the world

This area of learning corresponds directly to what is called in the Montessori classroom the cultural area. The activities in this area focus on biology, geography, history and science. Here the Montessori early years curriculum consists of a range of teacher-made materials, often developed in conjunction with topics or projects introduced to the classroom. These topics and projects are often negotiated with the children and should reflect the children's interests and fascinations. The focus is, whenever possible, on real experiences that enhance and complement learning through the senses, so appropriate for this age group.

All Montessori classrooms should have plants and flowers both inside and outside in the garden. They are often part of the nature table that reflects 'finds and discoveries' during nature walks and from the garden. They also give opportunities for children to bring items into the classroom that they have found during walks with their parents or on the way to school – such as conkers, leaves, snails and so on. The nature table serves as a focus for observation, exploration and investigation. Real experiences are complemented by access to books, pictures and teacher-made materials. The nature table usually reflects the topics or projects and may relate to work on transport, my body, minibeast, volcanoes, continents, solar system as well as more abstract themes such as electricity, magnetism or light.

The sense of time is introduced with the help of a range of time lines and life cycles, and by regular use of calendars. Birthdays are celebrated and also contribute to the children's understanding of the passage of time.

Learning about places is approached from a unique perspective in Montessori classrooms as the child becomes aware of the solar system and the planet Earth and its continents long before they come to study the country in which they were born. This is part of the Montessori ethos and focuses on giving children the opportunity of becoming 'citizens of the world'.

Montessori teachers introduce continents from a multi-sensory perspective, first by looking at the globe and then by working with the puzzle map of the world that identifies each continent by its unique colour. Collections of objects and pictures from each continent are contained within artefact boxes and give children opportunities to explore each continent through its music, clothes, food, plants and animals as well as festivals and geographical features. The boxes are fundamental in bringing the lives and cultures of different continents into the classroom and, by doing so, promoting multicultural awareness and respect.

Designing and making skills are developed and encouraged through activities such as carpentry and craft and other activities in the practical life area. In this aspect of learning, Montessori teachers observe children, discuss their ideas and make resources available to ensure that children have opportunities to develop their design ideas.

There are many Montessori classrooms that include a computer as part of their resources available to the children within the aspect of information and communication technology. However, debate continues within the Montessori community as to the value of computers, particularly if they take over from the real experiences of life.

For example the experience of feeling the texture of a leaf or shell, smelling a flower, or feeling the wetness of a snail slithering along the arm cannot be replaced by seeing computer images. On the other hand the children have everyday technology available to them in the practical life area, such as scales, a grinder and graters, sticky tape dispenser, telephones, tape recorders and digital cameras. If these are available they are functioning objects rather than models or replicas. Many Montessori classrooms have also invested in a range of programmable toys.

Physical development

Physical development is inherent in all the activities carried out in the Montessori classroom. Small children learning by doing, and therefore manipulation is a key strategy for learning.

Movement consists of gross and fine motor skills, awareness of space and balance. These are part of the daily life of the Montessori classroom; children choose activities, carry them to their workspace, work with them and put them away. They need to plan where they want to do their chosen activities and have to negotiate the space available to them. Once settled in their workspace, either on the floor or at a table, they have the opportunity to repeat an activity and perfect the given skill. Montessori saw very close links between motor skills and brain development, calling the hand the 'instrument of man's intelligence' (Montessori, 1988a:127). Manipulation and refinement of movement is encouraged by the use of a range of equipment, tools and materials.

Here we have the opportunity to make cross-curricular links primarily between physical and creative development and knowledge and understanding of the world. From the Montessori point of view all the Montessori curriculum areas contribute to the refinement of the child's movement with special and unique contribution made by both practical life and sensorial areas. This learning may take place indoors as well as outdoors, as Montessori was a great advocate for outdoor learning and recognised the importance of what we call today the outdoor classroom. Music and movement activities also contribute to this area of learning.

Health and bodily awareness are once again part of everyday activities within the classroom as they become part of the daily routine, particularly during meal times and outdoor activities. Special projects devoted to 'my body' or 'myself' will also reflect this aspects of the foundation curriculum. Many Montessori nurseries are committed to healthy eating programmes and regulate the food offered to children by the nursery or brought into the nursery from home.

Creative development

This area of learning provides children with opportunities to develop both their physical skills as well as their imagination. This area of leaning in the Montessori classrooms has come under criticism in the past, but current training of Montessori teachers has addressed this component of the curriculum. The emphasis on creativity helps children develop skill in using resources spontaneously and gives opportunities for development of the imagination, with support from the adults in the classroom.

This area of development has significant links with the sensorial materials area, particularly if we understand the child's creativity to be the ability to use their imagination.

Exploration of media and materials relates particularly to use of arts and crafts materials, musical instruments and drama props, such as puppets and objects from story sacks. All these are available in Montessori classrooms and usually children have the opportunity to access them during the three-hour work cycle rather than during organised lesson. However, in addition to the spontaneous use, some nurseries also employ a specialist teacher who gives more formal lesson once a week in the areas of their expertise, such as music, art, craft or drama.

Singing is part of the daily routine of Montessori classrooms, and musical instruments are also available, usually under supervision of the teacher. Movement often becomes an integral part of the music lessons as children act out song and demonstrate specific movement; usually this is the first introduction to drama. Children also have opportunities to listen to a variety of music, such as music from different continents, folk, jazz or classical music.

It is not very common to see role play areas designed by teachers in the Montessori classrooms. This does not mean that children are not given the opportunity to develop their imagination, but it is more likely that role play scenarios will evolve spontaneously and will reflect the children's own experiences of life. This approach relies on the adults' observation skills and good range of resources to facilitate role play as it emerges. The adult involvement is essential, if opportunities to facilitate children's use of imagination are not to be missed.

In a way all that happens in the classroom requires the opportunity for children and adults to be engaged in a dialogue. They need to be given time to express and communicate their ideas in a chosen medium, be it in painting, drawing, modelling, carpentry, blocks, dance, singing and playing an instrument, role play or gardening. Creativity is present in all that children do in the classroom.

Please see Appendix 1 for the specific ways a Montessori nursery meets the early learning goals. This information may be given to parents when their children start nursery and serves as the framework for planning and record keeping. It identifies the individual learning goals.

Appendix 1

How the early learning goals are met at a Montessori nursery

Personal, social and emotional development

Early learning goal	Montessori practice
Disposition and attitude	
Children:	Children:
■ continue to be interested, exited and motivated to learn	■ are helped to settle into the routine of the classroom; ■ do accessible activities; ■ are encouraged to make choices; ■ have 'how the classroom works' explained to them;
■ are confident to try new activities, initiate ideas and speak in a familiar group;	■ select activities spontaneously; ■ are curious about new activities introduced by teachers and are ready to try them; ■ contribute to discussions at circle time, around nature table, in book corner when sharing activities with the group;
■ maintain attention, concentrate and sit quietly when appropriate.	■ concentrate when working on a self-chosen activity; ■ are involved when working within a group; ■ are able to listen to a story; ■ begin meditation in yoga; ■ are able to listen to explanations.
Self-confidence and self-esteem	
■ respond to significant experiences, showing a range of feelings when appropriate;	■ have their responses recorded in an anecdotal format by teachers, where appropriate;

Early learning goal	Montessori practice
■ have a developing awareness of their own needs, views and feelings and be sensitive to the needs, views and feelings of others;	■ are encouraged to take part in discussions and negotiations; ■ are allowed to show their needs, views and feelings when these present themselves;
■ have a developing respect for their own cultures and beliefs and those of other people.	■ discuss and develop a growing awareness of other cultures through projects.

Making relationships

■ form good relationships with adults and peers;	■ are able to settle well in the mornings; ■ are able to share ideas, food, toys and materials with peers and adults in nursery; ■ show politeness and consideration for friends, peers and adults;
■ work as part of a group or a class, taking turns and sharing fairly, understanding that there need to be agreed values and codes of behaviour for groups of people, including adults and children, to work together harmoniously.	■ are able to gradually accept the principles of sharing and caring for the classroom so that it can be used freely by everyone.

Behaviour and self-control

■ understand what is right, what is wrong, and why;	■ are able to follow the expected code of behaviour and learn about why this is important;
■ consider the consequences of their words and actions for themselves and others.	■ learn about the consequences of behaviour, spoken word and actions.

Self-care

■ dress and undress independently and manage their own personal hygiene;	■ have a growing ability to put on a coat to go outside/home, use the toilet and wash their hands after using the toilet and before eating a snack or lunch; ■ know about personal hygiene such as cleaning their teeth, brushing hair and so on;
■ select and use activities and resources independently.	■ are able to use the prepared environment fully, working in all areas, alone and with friends.

Early learning goal	Montessori practice
Sense of community	
■ understand that people have different needs, views, cultures and beliefs that need to be treated with respect;	■ take part in discussions during circle time, but also as incidents occur in nursery; ■ learn to put activities away so that they are ready for others; ■ do project work on festivals, people and animals of the world;
■ understand that they can expect others to treat their needs, views, cultures and beliefs with respect.	■ have teachers who are role models; ■ show respect for each others' work; ■ show general respect and polite behaviour towards each other.

Communication, language and literacy

Early learning goal	Montessori practice
Communication	
Children:	Children:
■ interact with others, negotiating plans and activities and taking turns in conversation;	■ have freedom of speech, circle time, a book corner and art area and play games such as animal lotto and participate in block play, role play and outdoor play;
■ enjoy listening to and using spoken and written language, and readily turn to it in their play and learning;	■ share books either on a one-to-one basis, in small groups or during circle time; ■ listen to guidance on how to use materials and participate in cooking and other activities;
■ sustain attentive listening, responding to what they have heard by relevant comments, questions or actions;	■ participate in story time and circle time and engage in attentive listening; ■ participate in the Silence Game, which invites them to listen carefully to sounds in the environment; ■ participate in I Spy and Odd Man Out games, which contribute to listening for initial sounds in words;
■ listen with enjoyment and respond to stories, songs and other music, rhymes and poems and make up their own stories, songs, rhymes and poems;	■ participate and enjoy listening to stories, children's freedom of choice to participate in activities is an important element in the enjoyment of all they do;

Early learning goal	Montessori practice
■ extend their vocabulary, exploring the meanings and sounds of new words;	■ have circle time and story time, make books, work with books on the project table and name objects in the environment and projects;
■ speak clearly and audibly with confidence and control and show awareness of the listener, for example by their use of conventions such as greetings, 'please' and 'thank you'.	■ participate at circle time, discuss at snack time and at the beginning of the day; ■ are polite role models and have expectations of polite behaviour from each other; ■ use language to negotiate 'what they would like or need'.

Thinking

■ use language to imagine and recreate roles and experiences;	■ have a 'farm area' or 'hospital' for small world play; ■ role play and play outdoors; ■ play with 'dinosaurs/other animals';
■ Use talk to organise, sequence and clarify thinking, ideas, feelings and events.	■ have block play, practical life, sensorial and role play areas; ■ negotiate during spontaneously chosen activities.

Linking sounds and letters

■ hear and say sounds in words in the order in which they occur;	■ work on games such as I Spy, Odd Man Out and word building with Large Movable Alphabet;
■ link sounds to letters, naming and sounding the letters of the alphabet;	■ match letters to the alphabet, recognise their own and other children's name by the initials, use the letter tray and letters made of sandpaper and play I Spy games;
■ use their phonic knowledge to write simple regular words and make phonetically plausible attempts at more complex words.	■ use word building with Large Movable Alphabet, write titles on artwork and make books and write their own ideas in them.

Reading

■ explore and experiment with sounds, words and text;	■ play rhyming games, 'onset and rime', label objects and own work and make books;
■ retell narratives in the correct sequence, drawing on language patterns of stories;	■ use puppets and props to retell stories or follow up on a story started by someone else;

Early learning goal	Montessori practice
■ read a range of familiar and common words and simple sentences independently;	■ label things in the classroom and read phrases and sentences;
■ know that print carries meaning and in English is read from left to right and top to bottom;	■ use and care for books competently and appropriate, enjoy using books and share books with teachers and peers;
■ show an understanding of the elements of stories, such as main character, sequence of events, and openings, and how information can be found in non-fiction texts to answer questions about where, who, why and how.	■ are encouraged to make up stories with the help of objects and 'write' stories with the help of pictures or objects from reading activities.

Writing

■ use their phonic knowledge to write simple regular words and make phonetically plausible attempts at more complex words;	■ word build with Large Moveable Alphabet; ■ write words, phrases, sentences in work books or on artwork;
■ attempt writing for different purposes, using features of different forms such as lists, stories and instructions;	■ use the writing area, start emergent writing, have opportunities to write in the role play area and write titles for paintings and drawings;
■ write their own names and other things such as labels and captions and begin to write simple sentences, sometimes using punctuation.	■ write their own name on paintings and illustrated workbooks.

Handwriting

■ use a pencil and hold it effectively to form recognisable letters, most of which are correctly formed.	■ are introduced to insets for design, have access to paints and craft area and are encouraged to form letters with sandpaper letters.

Mathematical development

Early learning goal	Montessori practice
Numbers as labels and for counting	
Children:	Children:
■ say and use numbers' names in order in a familiar context;	■ join in rhymes and use counting books and count shoes, the number of children present and days of the week;
■ count reliably up to ten everyday objects;	■ count number rods, pegs, spindles, counters and other objects in the environment;
■ recognise numerals 1 to 9;	■ use sandpaper numerals and a spindle box, number cards, birthday display and calendar;
■ use developing mathematical ideas and methods to solve practical problems.	■ play the Snake Game to make number bonds of ten, play dominoes, and make symmetrical, regular and irregular structures; ■ are helped to find out what happens if objects are organised in pairs or sets or taken away.
Calculating	
■ in practical activities and discussions, begin to use the vocabulary involved in adding and subtracting;	■ are introduced to the concept of addition and subtraction within everyday activities in the classroom, such as artwork and building with blocks;
■ use language such as 'more' or 'less' to compare two numbers;	■ count the number of spoons or raisins or biscuits taken at snack time or lunch time and count in the context of everyday activities such as circle time or going outside; ■ are introduced to the appropriate language in the context of everyday activities;
■ find one more or one less than a number from one to ten;	■ use a number line, short bead stairs and the addition and subtraction strip board to count and explore numbers;
■ begin to relate addition to combining two groups of objects and subtraction to 'taking away'.	■ are introduced to the Snake Game and addition and subtraction with short bead stairs and play counting games such as Greengrocers.

Early learning goal	Montessori practice
Shape, space and measures	
■ use language such as 'greater', 'smaller', 'heavier' or 'lighter' to compare quantities;	■ use and compare sensorial materials to explore length, height, width and depth; ■ use appropriate vocabulary in everyday context, such as when cooking, setting table or gardening;
■ talk about, recognise and recreate simple patterns;	■ use of tessellations and constructive triangles and materials (such as collage) in the art area to make patterns; ■ do puzzles and work with unit blocks;
■ use language such as 'circle' or 'bigger' to describe the shape and size of solids and flat shapes;	■ use geometric solids, the geometric cabinet and binomial and trinomial cubes;
■ use everyday words to describe position;	■ play mapping games, play with blocks and play outdoor games in the playground and during music and movement activities;
■ use developing mathematical ideas and methods to solve practical problems.	■ prepare for group activities such as cooking, measuring, role play and 'organising the farm'; ■ use a variety of materials to explore patterns, tessellations, tap-tap it and pegs.

Knowledge and understanding of the world

Early learning goal	Montessori practice
Exploration and investigation	
Children:	Children:
■ investigate objects and materials by using all of their senses as appropriate;	■ do project work, work at the nature table displays, science, gardening and plant activities;
■ find out about, and identify, some features of living things, objects and events they observe;	■ do project work and have discussions in relation to activities available in the cultural area of the classroom;
■ look closely at similarities, differences, patterns and change;	■ find out about life cycles and the needs of plants and people; ■ learn about the consequences of science activities;

Early learning goal	Montessori practice
◼ ask questions about why things happen and how things work.	◼ have opportunities for asking questions that come out of work on displays on the nature table and individual and group work with activities presented within projects.

Designing and making

◼ build and construct with a wide range of objects, selecting appropriate resources, and adapting their work where necessary;	◼ use block play and model making and have access to carpentry, all contribute to their ability to design and make 3D objects and constructions;
◼ select the tools and techniques they need to shape, assemble and join materials with which they are working.	◼ have access to a Craft area that is always set up with a wide rage of resources both for art and craft and for making things, facilitating of children's requests for making things such as rockets and masks.

Information and communication technology

◼ find out about and identify the uses of everyday technology and use information and communication technology and programmable toys to support their learning.	◼ make use of a tape recorder and story tapes; ◼ can use a typewriter; ◼ make use of a telephone; ◼ are introduced to a variety of programmable toys such as Pixie; ◼ use technology such as mixers, beaters, hammers and screwdrivers for cooking and for repairs.

Sense of time

◼ find out about past and present events in their lives and in those of their families and other people they know.	◼ discuss what is important to them; ◼ discuss the calendar and seasons; ◼ discuss life cycles and make time lines; ◼ explore photographs.

Sense of place

◼ observe, find out about and identify features in the place they live and the natural world;	◼ observe and explore the garden; ◼ talk about where they live and where things are and the places we use and visit such as supermarkets, the library, the museum and the market place;
◼ find out about their environment and talk about those features they like and dislike.	◼ discuss the walks to the playground; ◼ make up a mapping game.

Early learning goal	Montessori practice
Cultures and beliefs	
■ begin to know about their own cultures and beliefs and those of other people.	■ celebrate birthdays and festivals; ■ talk about different cultures in relation to the dressing up box.

Physical development

Early learning goal	Montessori practice
Movement	
Children:	Children:
■ move with confidence, imagination and in safety;	■ learn music and movement, use outdoor equipment in the garden and regularly visit the playground;
■ move with control and coordination;	■ do yoga, play Who's Afraid of Mr Wolf? use bicycles, garden and use the snack and art areas;
■ travel around, under, over and through balancing and climbing equipment.	■ use bicycles and the tunnel for climbing and crawling; ■ play Walking on the Line games and use the climbing apparatus in the playground.
Sense of space	
■ show awareness of space, of themselves and of others.	■ use the classroom and outdoor space during free play.
Health and bodily awareness	
■ recognise the importance of keeping healthy and those things that contribute to this;	■ are offered healthy snacks, talk about food during lunchtime, do project work on food and its benefits;
■ recognise the changes that happen to their bodies when they are active.	■ do project work on how our body works, what it does, what makes it healthy and who helps us to keep it healthy.
Using equipment	
■ use a range of small and large equipment.	■ use the practical life and outdoor areas to do gardening, carpentry, art activities and cooking.

Early learning goal	Montessori practice
Using tools and materials	
■ handle tools, objects, construction and malleable materials safely and with increasing control.	■ in the practical life area have access to tools and objects that develop fine movements and control.

Creative development

Early learning goal	Montessori practice
Exploring media and materials	
Children:	Children:
■ explore colour, texture, shape, form and space in two and three dimensions.	■ do art and craft work and work with blocks and modelling; ■ do spontaneous and planned activities.
Music	
■ recognise and explore how sounds can be changed, sing simple songs from memory, recognise repeated sounds and sound patterns and match movement to music.	■ do daily singing, which offers children the opportunity to share their songs, as a group or individually; ■ participate in weekly music and movement sessions; ■ play music games.
Imagination	
■ use their imagination in art and design, music dance, imaginative and role play and stories.	■ have free expression in art and craft activities; ■ dance to music, participate in organised and spontaneous role play, use prepared and spontaneously chosen props; ■ listen to storytelling that is linked to painting; ■ do practical life activities when block building, playing with the farm, dolls house or hospital, during dressing up and when in the garden.
Responding to experiences, and expressing and communication ideas	
■ respond in a variety of ways to what they see, hear, smell touch and feel;	■ refine their senses through the sensorial materials and outdoor activities such as exploration of the garden, nature walks and gardening;

Early learning goal	Montessori practice
■ express and communicate their ideas, thoughts and feelings by using a widening range of materials, suitable tools, imaginative and role play, movement, designing and making, and a variety of songs and musical instruments.	■ express their ideas and thoughts during practical life, sensorial, literacy, maths activities; ■ discuss ideas, feelings and thoughts about a given topic; ■ do spontaneous role play, stimulated by practical life, during outdoor activities and in the cultural area; ■ do organised role play that is linked to specific project work,

Montessori activities and materials

These materials provide learning opportunities for children between the ages of three to six years.

Practical life

Coordinated movement

■ pouring, with jugs, small containers, strainers, funnels;

■ transferring, with spoons, scoops, tongs, pipettes, droppers;

■ estimating, sorting and matching.

These activities develop wrist flexibility, fine motor skills, eye–hand coordination, dexterity.

Opening and closing

■ opening a variety of containers, including those in the activity areas in the classroom;

■ opening boxes, bottle lids;

■ undoing padlocks, nuts, bolts.

These activities develop wrist flexibility (useful in writing).

Classroom skills

■ cutting, using a variety of narrow paper strips;

■ threading, using a range of beads from large to small;

- sewing, using sewing cards initially and progressing to use of a needle and thread;

- plaiting, using different colours of cord to highlight the pattern of the plait;

- folding, to make an envelope or book, to wrap a parcel, to fold cloths and clothes used in the classroom;

- using glue, paper clips, stapler, hole punch, date stamp.

These activities develop fine motor movement, particularly a pincer grip (useful in writing and art).

Personal independence and hygiene

- washing hands;

- using the toilet;

- cleaning teeth;

- using the nail brush;

- putting on a coat;

- putting on shoes or wellingtons;

- using a dressing frame to do up and undo buttons, laces, bows, buckles, zips.

These activities help develop skills of everyday classroom participation.

Contributing towards upkeep of the classroom

- washing, scrubbing tables and chairs, washing dusters, washing dishes (after snack or lunch);

- polishing, glass, brass, silver, wood, mirror, shoes;

- sweeping, dusting, wiping tables;

- setting the table for lunch or snack;

- gardening and looking after plants and pets.

These activities develop dexterity and contribute towards social awareness and a sense of well being (as the child helps to look after the classroom).

The senses

The materials listed below can:

- refine sensorial impressions gathered during the early days of life and help organise and classify them;

- be used for matching, pairing, sorting, sequencing (laying foundations for later work in mathematics);

- help develop understanding of one-to-one correspondence, seriation and patterns and prepare for study of geometry and algebra (by understanding shape and form);

- develop dexterity and eye–hand coordination;

- help develop understanding of two- and three-dimensional shapes (by feeling them) and appreciation of shapes and forms found in our environment.

Understanding of shape, size and their relationships

- knobbed cylinders;

- pink tower;

- broad stair;

- long rods;

- coloured cylinders.

Chromatic sense

- colour boxes: colour box 1 includes pairs of the primary colours; colour box 2 includes eleven pairs of colours; colour box 3 includes nine colours.

Understanding of geometry and algebra

- geometric solids and their bases, stereognostic bags;

- the presentation tray, geometric cabinet and cards' constructive triangles, tessellations;

- binomial and trinomial cube.

Activities to refine tactile sense

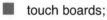 touch boards;

■ touch tablets;

■ touch fabrics.

Activities to refine understanding of weight

 baric tablets.

Activities to refine understanding of temperature

■ thermic tablets;

■ thermic bottles.

Activities to refine auditory sense

■ sound boxes;

■ Montessori bells.

Activities to refine the sense of smell

■ smell bottles.

Activities to refine the sense of taste

■ taste jars.

Mathematics

Children work with numbers, exploring both quantities and symbols, before being introduced to the decimal system and addition, subtraction, multiplication and division.

Counting 0–10

The child builds up an understanding of 0 to 10 by manipulating objects and associating these objects with the written symbol. The child begins to learn one-to-one correspondence and the sequential nature of numbers.

- large number rods;
- sandpaper numerals;
- number rods and cards;
- spindle box;
- cards and counters.

The decimal system

Golden beads (which can be replaced by the wooden decimal materials commercially produced) are used to introduce the hierarchies of the decimal system. Beads as well as numeral cards (which use colour to represent the given hierarchies and place value) are used.

Group operations with golden beads

These activities introduce addition, subtractions, multiplication and division through group games.

They reinforce knowledge of numbers to 10 and relationships of decimal hierarchies. They introduce the concept of changing from one decimal hierarchy to another.

They provide a tangible example of the principles behind the four operations, for example, that addition is a process in which we 'add several smaller quantities to make another, larger quantity'.

Counting 10 to 99

- Teen Boards (Seguin Board A) numbers 11–19 using new materials;
- Ten Boards (Seguin Board B) numbers 10–99 using new materials;
- bead chains 100/1000 conservation/reversibility of number.

Addition and subtraction of small numbers (1 to 19)

Addition activities

- Snake Game (number bonds to 10);
- number rods (addition equations);

- addition with short bead stair (recording answers);
- addition strip board – introducing adding on, practising recording.

Subtraction activities

- subtraction with short bead stair (subtraction equations);
- small number rods (recording answers).

Tables

Children start working on tables, still using objects that they manipulate.

Charts

These charts reinforce previous learning of the number operations and help children memorise answers to the equation.

- addition chart A and B;
- subtraction chart A and B;
- multiplication chart A and B;
- division chart A and B.

Fractions

Children start to use the fraction materials, using the fraction symbols and combining them with the fraction pieces. They learn about numerators, denominators, equivalents and reduction.

Measurement

Children learn about measurement by using spoons, cups as well as scales to measure ingredients during cooking activities.

They also use the long rods as a unit of measurement and usually have access to a measuring tape.

They learn about clocks and time recognition is usually introduced around the age of five.

Money is introduced during role play.

Literacy materials

Most of the literacy materials used are teacher-made.

Writing

- Insets of design encourage pencil control, lightness of touch and contribute to letter formation.

- Sandpaper letters introduce the child to letter sounds and shapes in a multi-sensory manner.

- Large Moveable Alphabets make links between the letter shape and formation of words at the time when children may not have the motor ability to write words. Objects and pictures are used to help children identify suitable words for word building.

Reading

Most Montessori nursery schools organise their reading activities into colour-coded levels, starting with words that consist of a consonant followed by a vowel followed by a consonant such as mat, pin, box. These words are suited to further activities with 'onset and rime' and prepare children well to decode more complex words using blends, diagrams and phonograms.

Pink level reading

The first level of reading focuses on three letter words consisting of the regular pattern consonant, vowel, consonant (such as pin, cot, bib).

Blue level reading

When children are competent in decoding three letters words, they are introduced to initial and final blends, the schwa vowel, double consonants (such as st, fr-, fl-, pr-, -ck, -sh, sh-, -ch, ch-, -th, th-).

Resources for children following the same sequence of activities in both levels:

- Boxes 1 and 2 – word building with Large Moveable Alphabet;

- Box 3 – decoding words on word cards using objects;

- Box 4 – supporting word cards with pictures;
- Box 5 – decoding without props (a mystery box);
- word lists;
- phrases;
- sentences;
- books.

Grammar

Grammar is introduced early in Montessori classrooms in support of the pink and blue level reading and with the help of colour-coding, which represents parts of speech.

Parts of speech are introduced through games, starting with nouns as labels that can be placed with objects in the classroom such as map, bin, rod.

- noun labels;
- singular and plural boxes, introducing the formation of plurals by adding -s;
- adjective labels;
- noun and adjective games, highlighting the function of adjectives and their position;
- verb games, acting out verbs;
- preposition boxes, highlighting the function of prepositions;
- farm boxes, building sentences based around the theme of a farm.

Green level reading

This level of reading requires competence at both the pink and blue levels. It focuses on one specific phonogram or diagraph such as -ar. The children work through the activities listed below before moving on to the next green box, which identifies new spellings.

- reading – supported by the use of pictures;
- word building – spelling difficulty is highlighted by the colour of letters, which represent the given phonogram or diagraph;

- word lists;
- phrases;
- sentences;
- books.

Cultural studies

Most of the cultural materials used in the Montessori classroom are teacher-made.

The globes and puzzle maps used in geography can be obtained from Montessori suppliers. These materials contribute to the child's greater understanding of the natural and created world and encourage observation, exploration and investigation.

Biology

- a nature table, reflecting the seasons and children's interests;
- models such as farm, wild and sea animals and birds;
- pictures or plants, animals, habitats in their classifications;
- terminology puzzles and cards identifying part of an animal or a plant;
- life cycles.

Geography

- land, air and water boxes;
- globes, showing land and water and the continents;
- land forms and cards;
- puzzle maps of the world and individual continents;
- animals of the world;
- flags;
- artefact boxes and collections of pictures of children and their families from around the world;
- mapping games.

History

Children are introduce to the concept of time.

 egg timers;

 time lines;

■ calendars.

Science

Experiments that focus on investigating the properties of:

■ the four elements (light, water, air, fire – fire is used with adult supervision only);

■ magnetism;

■ electricity.

Bibliography

Bowlby, J. (1988) *Secure Base.* London: Penguin.

Britton, L. (1998) *Montessori: Play and Learn.* New York: Vermillion Press.

Bruce, T. (1991) *Time to Play in Early Childhood Education.* London: Hodder and Stoughton.

Bruce, T. (2005) *Early Childhood Education*, 3rd edn. London: Hodder Arnold.

Bruner, J. (1960) *The Process of Education.* Cambridge, MA: Harvard University Press.

Chattin-McNichols, J. (1992) *The Montessori Controversy.* New York: Delmar Publishers Inc.

Duffy, M. and Duffy, D. (2002) *Children of the Universe, Cosmic Education in the Montessori Elementary Classroom.* Hollidaysburgh, PA: Parent Child Press.

Gettman, D. (1987) *Basic Montessori, Learning Activities for Under-Fives.* Oxford: ABC Clio Ltd.

Gura, P. ed. (1992) *Exploring Learning: Young Children and Blockplay.* London: Paul Chapman.

Hainstock, E. (1978) *Essential Montessori.* New York: Plume Books.

Holt, J. (1967) *How Children Learn.* London: Penguin.

Jenkinson, S. (2002) *The Genius of Play.* Stroud: Hawthorn Press.

Kelly, A. V. (1989) *The Curriculum, Theory and Practice.* London: Paul Chapman Publishing Ltd.

Kramer, R. (1976) *Maria Montessori.* London: Montessori International Publishing.

Lawrence, L. (1998) *Montessori: Read and Write.* London: Ebury Press.

Liebeck, P. (1984) *How Children Learn Mathematics*. London: Penguin.

Lillard, P. P. (1972) *Montessori, a Modern Approach*. New York: Schocken Books.

Lillard, P. P. (1980) *Montessori in the Classroom*. New York: Schocken Books.

Lillard, P. P. (1996) *Montessori Today*. New York: Schocken Books.

Lillard, P. P. and Lillard, L. L. (2003) *Montessori from the Start*. New York: Schocken Books.

Loeffler, M. H. ed. (1992) *Montessori in Contemporary American Culture*. Portsmouth, NH: Heinemann.

Macleod-Brudenell, I. ed. (2004) *Advanced Early Years Care and Education*. Oxford: Heinemann.

MCI, Montessori Centre International (2006) *Montessori Philosophy, Module 1*. London: MCI.

Montanaro, S. Q. (1991) *Understanding the Human Being*. Mountain View, CA: Nienhuis Montessori USA.

Montessori, M. (1964) [1912] *The Montessori Method*. New York: Schocken Books.

Montessori, M. (1965) [1914] *Dr Montessori's Own Handbook*. New York: Schocken Books.

Montessori, M. (1966) [1936] *The Secret of Childhood*. Notre Dame, IN: Fides Publishers Ltd.

Montessori, M. (1988a) [1949] *The Absorbent Mind*. Oxford: ABC – Clio Ltd, Volume 1.

Montessori, M. (1988b) [1912] *The Discovery of the Child* (originally published as *The Montessori Method*). Oxford: ABC – Clio Ltd, Volume 2.

Montessori, M. (1989a) [1955] *The Formation of Man*. Oxford: ABC – Clio Ltd, Volume 3.

Montessori, M. (1989b) [1961] *What You Should Know About Your Child*. Oxford: ABC – Clio Ltd, Volume 4.

Montessori, M. (1989c) [1946] *Education for New World*. Oxford: ABC – Clio Ltd, Volume 5.

Montessori, M. (1989d) [1948] *To Educate the Human Potential*. Oxford: ABC – Clio Ltd, Volume 6.

Montessori, M. (1989e) [1979] *The Child, Society and the World.* Oxford: ABC – Clio Ltd, Volume 7.

Montessori, M. (1989f) [1975] *The Child in the Family.* Oxford: ABC – Clio Ltd, Volume 8.

Montessori, M. (1991) [1918] *The Advanced Montessori Method – Volume 1.* Oxford: ABC – Clio Ltd, Volume 9.

Montessori, M. (1992) [1949] *Education and Peace.* Oxford: ABC – Clio Ltd, Volume 10.

Montessori, M. (1994) [1948] *From Childhood and Adolescence.* Oxford: ABC – Clio Ltd, Volume 12.

Montessori, M. (1995) [1916] *The Advanced Montessori Method – Volume 2.* Oxford: ABC – Clio Ltd, Volume 13.

Montessori, M. (1997a) [1976] *Basic Ideas of Montessori's Educational Theory.* Oxford: ABC – Clio Ltd, Volume 14.

Montessori, M. (1997b) *California Lectures of Maria, 1915.* Oxford: ABC – Clio Ltd, Volume 15.

Montessori, M. Jnr (1992) [1976] *Education for Human Development.* Oxford: ABC – Clio Ltd, Volume 11.

Moyles, J. ed. (2005) *Excellence of Play.* Buckingham/Philadelphia, PA: Open University Press.

Piaget, J. (1962) *Play, Dreams and Imitation in Childhood.* London: Routledge & Kegan Paul.

QCA and DfES (2000) *Curriculum Guidance for the Foundation Stage.* London: QCA.

Rich, D. *et al.* (2005) *First Hand Experience: What Matters to Children: An Alphabet of Learning from the Real World.* London: Rich Learning Opportunities.

Standing E. M. (1984) *Maria Montessori, Her Life and Work.* New York: Plume.

Stoll-Lillard, A. (2004) *The Science Behind the Genius.* New York: Oxford University Press Inc.

Vygostsky, L. (1978) *Mind in Society.* Cambridge, MA: Harvard University Press.

Wolf, A. D. (1996) *Nurturing the Spirit in Non-sectarian Classrooms.* Hollidaysburg, PA: Parent Child Press.